STORIES AND GAMES

FOR

EASY LIPREADING PRACTICE

by

Rose Feilbach Broberg

The Alexander Graham Bell Association for the Deaf, Inc.
Headquarters: The Volta Bureau
1537 35th Street, N. W.
Washington, D.C. 20007, U.S.A.

Printed and Bound in U. S. A.

CONTENTS

GAMES, QUIZZES, AND PUPIL READINGS

Page

TRUE STORIES AND LEGENDS

ANECDOTES

PREFACE

This book -- like the average TV program or the average movie -- has been planned for use with either children or adults. Whether the pupil be a precocious fourth grader or the breadwinner of the family, either one can enjoy these "average" productions.

Most adults will find the material interesting. Junior and senior high school pupils relished most of the materia and even took some of it back to the classrooms with them Elementary school children above the third grade can be given a large part of the material, provided it is simplified. Some of the selections are easy enough as they are written. The success of any lipreading lesson will always depend largely on the personality of the teacher, anyhow!

Where acknowledgment is not given for any particular story or anecdote, remember that Joe Miller probably sired it. In fact, we have collected humorous stories for so many years -- by word of mouth, by scraps of sentences written on the backs of old envelopes, by key word scribbled on the sides of conference programs -- that we would fear to make any attempt at direct acknowledgments.

On the Farm - - - a Quiz

Give one point to each person who is first with the correct answer. The one who gains the most points wins the game.

1.   Give me the names of four animals that live on a farm.

2.   Can you name three tools that a farmer uses on a farm?

3.   Name three things that a farmer plants.

4.   Can you draw a picture of a barn?

5.   Can you draw a picture of a dog house?

6.   What do we call the place where the pigs live?

7.   Where do bees make their honey?

8.   What do we call a farm where they raise all kinds of fruit trees?

9.   What do we call a farm where they raise cows for beef?

10. What do we call the place where the horses sleep?

Food, Clothing, or Shelter ?

The above three headings are to be written at the top of the blackboard. The teacher reads the sentences. When the pupil understands the sentence and knows under which designation it is to be placed, he comes to the blackboard and writes the name of the article in the proper column. He then repeats the sentence aloud to the class.

1. All of us should drink three glasses of <u>milk</u> every day.

2. My mother bought the baby a new pair of <u>shoes</u>.

3. My brother is building a ranch-type <u>house</u>.

4. We passed fields of <u>cotton</u> when we drove through the South.

5. When it is very cold, my mother wears a fur <u>coat</u>.

6. Abraham Lincoln was born in a <u>log cabin</u>.

7. The farmer planted <u>potatoes</u>.

8. When I went to camp last summer, I slept in a <u>pup tent</u>.

9. The butcher sold me some <u>hamburger</u>.

10. The boys played in a <u>cave</u> in the mountains.

11. This large <u>grapefruit</u> came from California.

12. Who is wearing a blue-striped <u>shirt</u>?

A Quiz on Washington and Lincoln

(Adapted from "The Instructor" magazine, Feb. 1941)

Each student will have a sentence which has been typed on a slip of paper. As he reads his sentence to the class, the group will indicate whether the statement is true or false.

1. Washington was born on February 22, 1932.   F

2. Washington's favorite subject was arithmetic.

    T

3. Abraham Lincoln's family was able to send him to a fine private school.   F

4. Lincoln was known as an interesting storyteller.

    T

5. Abe Lincoln married Ann Rutledge.   F

6. Washington worked as a clerk in a country store.

    F

7. Washington was chosen President because of his fine character.   T

8. Lincoln was elected President for a second term.

    T

9. Lincoln is known as the Father of our Country.

    F

10. Lincoln tried hard to prevent a civil war.   T

11. Washington helped his father to build a log cabin for the family.   F

12. Abraham Lincoln had no children.   F

13. John Adams was Vice-President for George Washington.   T

14. George Washington's home was at Mt. Vernon.   T

15. Lincoln once made a speech we call "The Gettysburg Address."   T

16. Abraham Lincoln once threw a silver dollar across the Potomac River.   F

Modern Housing

(The instructor might preface this story by showing a picture of Washington's home at Mt. Vernon.)

A teacher had a class of first graders in a New York city school. She was talking to them about George Washington. Some of the children had brought in pictures. One child's mother had sent a picture of Mt. Vernon. The teacher held it up for the group to see.

She said, "This is where George Washington lived."

One little fellow stared at the picture for some time. Then he piped up, "On what floor?"

1. What grade was the teacher teaching?

2. In what city was the school?

3. What man was she talking about?

4. What kind of picture did one child bring in?

5. What did the teacher say about this picture?

6. Who asked the teacher a question about the picture?

7. What did he want to know?

Do You Know Your Presidents?

For this game the teacher will prepare slips of paper to distribute, each one bearing a number and one of the following questions. Each student will read his slip in front of the class. The class may be divided into two teams. Whichever team gets the most correct answers wins the game.

1. What President invented the ice-cream freezer?
   Washington

2. What President played golf in the snow with golf balls that were painted red?   Wilson

3. What President was a haberdasher?
   Truman

4. What President never went to school in all his life but was taught to read and write by his wife?

   Johnson

5. What President was only 26 years old when he became president of a college?

Garfield

6. What President had to have special bathtubs put in the White House because the ones already there were much too small for him?

Taft

7. What President failed to show up for his own wedding but later married the same girl in a big rush?

Lincoln

8. What President lived in England when he was a young man and had a home there called "White House"?

Hoover

9. What President married a woman with the same last name as his own?

F. D. Roosevelt

10. What President was so thrifty that he did all his own marketing while he lived at the White House?

Jefferson

11. What President was the first one to ride in an automobile?

McKinley

12. What President was a bachelor when he came into the White House and never was married?

Buchanan

13. What President was the first to announce that milk would be served at every meal in the White House?

J. F. Kennedy

The Professions of the Chief Executives

(Adapted from "Youth Today")

Who is the President of the United States? He is called the Chief Executive. What was his profession before he became President? Would you like to be President of the United States? What kind of profession will you follow? Perhaps you should be a lawyer. More than half of our Presidents have been lawyers.

There were 24 lawyers. John Adams was the second President of the United States. He was the first President who was a lawyer. Most of the lawyer Presidents studied law when they were very young. One President was only 19 when he finished his law work. He was Martin Van Buren.

Seven of our Presidents were teachers. They were teachers at one time or another in their lives. Two of the Presidents who were teachers were Grover Cleveland and James Garfield.

There were 16 Presidents who served in the Army. Only four of them made the Army their career. They were Benjamin Harrison, Zachary Taylor, Ulysses Grant and Dwight Eisenhower.

Some of our Presidents were once engineers. One President was a mining engineer. That was Herbert Hoover. One was a civil engineer. That was George Washington.

Andrew Johnson was a tailor. However, he spent most of his life in politics. Another President was a politician by profession. That was Theodore Roosevelt.

One President was a newspaper man. That was Warren Harding.

There was no President who remained a farmer by vocation. All the boys who had been farmers left the farm and became lawyers.

There were also no firemen, no policemen, no butchers, no bakers, no doctors, and no sailors among our Presidents.

You must know something about government if you want to be President. The President of the United States is usually chosen from a group that knows the most about government. The people who know the most about government are the ones who are best fitted to run the government.

Washington Did Without These Things

George Washington was one of the richest men in the United States. Although he had plenty of money he had to do without many things that we consider common today. Here are a few of the things he never had.

George Washington never had

> a fountain pen
> a telephone
> a radio
> a flashlight
> a safety match
> a typewriter
> a bicycle
> a concrete highway
> an ice cream cone
> a sewing machine

He never rode
           an elevator
           an escalator
           an automobile
           a street car
           an airplane

Can you mention some other things he did without?

The Chase

A certain man was very near-sighted. One day he went for a walk in the country. It was a very windy day. All of a sudden a strong gust of wind came along and blew off his hat.

The man started to chase his hat. While he was trying to get his hat, a woman came out of a nearby farmhouse. The woman shouted at the man.

"What are you doing there?" she screamed.

"I'm running after my hat," replied the man.

"That's not your hat," said the woman. "That's our little black hen that you're chasing."

1. What kind of vision did the man have?
2. Where did he go for a walk?
3. What kind of weather was it?
4. What happened to his hat?
5. While he was trying to chase his hat, who came out of a farmhouse?
6. What did the woman shout at him?
7. How did the man reply?
8. How did the woman prove that the man was near-sighted?

The Jefferson Memorial

(The teacher should be sure to have a picture of the
Memorial and perhaps one of the statue of Thomas
Jefferson to show the class. It would be well to have
the quotations written on the blackboard before starting the discussion.)

Thomas Jefferson was the third Presi-
dent of the United States. He was the first Secretary
of State. He wrote the Declaration of Independence.
He was the Governor of Virginia, not only once, but
twice. He was the founder of the University of Virginia.

Thomas Jefferson was a born architect.
He often called the Roman style the most perfect type
of building. His favorite style of building was the
circular or domed type. His home at Monticello has
the domed roof. The University of Virginia Rotunda
was designed by Jefferson. It also has the domed roof.
The Jefferson Memorial is adapted from this building.

The Jefferson Memorial is in Washington,
D. C. This Memorial was dedicated on April 13, 1943.
That was the 200th anniversary of Thomas Jefferson's
birth. The Memorial is very impressive. It is one
of the most impressive sights in the capital of the
United States.

The Jefferson Memorial is made of beautiful
white marble. It is surrounded by Japanese cherry
trees. The Memorial is reflected in the waters of the
Washington Tidal Basin.

The dome of the Memorial is of heavy
stone. It is 82 feet in diameter. Beneath it, there is
a framework of steel. The whole dome is covered by
a patterned marble roof.

The front portico faces the White House. Above this portico there is a sculptured group. This sculpture shows Jefferson standing at a table for the signing of the Declaration of Independence. On his right side are Benjamin Franklin and John Adams; on his left are Roger Sherman and Robert Livingston.

Inside the memorial is a statue of Thomas Jefferson. The statue is 19 feet high. It was designed by Rudulph Evans of New York. Because of the war, the first statue in the memorial was made of plaster. After the war, it was cast in bronze. The statue stands on a marble pedestal in the center of the memorial.

There are four entrances to the memorial. Above each entrance inside the memorial is a large panel. Each panel bears some of Jefferson's words in bronze letters. One panel starts: "We hold these truths to be self-evident---." Another panel starts: "God who gave us life gave us liberty---." A third panel starts: "Almighty God hath created the mind free---." The fourth panel starts: "I am not an advocate for frequent changes in laws and constitutions---."

As a symbol of Jefferson's democracy, the four entrances to the memorial face the four points of the compass. They will never be closed by bars or gates.

The Jefferson Memorial cost almost three million dollars.

Word Squares

Four-blocked squares are drawn on the blackboard.
The teacher reads a sentence and the pupil watches
for the last word. The pupil must repeat the whole
sentence to the class before he fills in the word horizontally in the square. This game may be played for
individual scoring or for team scoring. When played
for team scoring, the team receives one point for
each line; five points are given if a team captures a
complete square.

1. I don't know how to spell that word.   Example:
    My brother lives in the state of Ohio.
    What time does the bell ring?
    Are you afraid of cats and dogs?

w	o	r	d
O	h	i	o
r	i	n	g
d	o	g	s

2. What song shall we sing?
    I just had a wonderful idea.
    A small salamander is called a newt.
    Please shut the outside gate.

3. The cows are on the farm.
    We had to drive miles to find a parking area.
    Will you please let me rest!
    The male bird was calling for his mate.

4. Shall we go to look for them?
    Is your mother at home?
    The girl's name is Emma.
    I'm hungry for a square meal.

5. What kind of flowers shall we try to grow?
    The little girls like to jump rope.
    The birthstone for October is the opal.
    I hope you are feeling very well.

6. Did you ever make a wish on a falling star?
   That toothpaste comes in a large tube.
   Come over to my house as soon as you're able.
   The fisherman bought a new rod and reel.

7. We must walk a block to the next bus stop.
   The printer knows how to set up type.
   Why did you leave the window open?
   The founder of Pennsylvania was William Penn.

8. Tomorrow's weather is supposed to be fair.
   The automobile had a broken axle.
   This medicine will cure your aches and ills.
   I'm going away to the mountains for a rest.

9. I'm very glad that you came.
   China is part of the continent of Asia.
   A woman who is not married is called a miss.
   If the word is not hard, it must be easy.

10. The room is as broad as it's long.
    I spilled the ink and it ran all over.
    The man who fiddled while Rome burned was Nero.
    Mary, Mary, quite contrary, how does your garden
    grow?

11. Please chop some wood for the fire.
    I have a splendid idea.
    When is the landlord coming for the rent?
    Mother is on a diet and must be careful what she
    eats.

12. A small burrowing animal without eyes is called
    a mole.
    The covered wagon was pulled by four oxen.
    My eyelids are as heavy as lead.
    I bought a pair of marble book ends.

A Few Facts About Some of

Our National Parks

(Adapted from "Scholastic" magazine, April 22, 1940)

The largest and oldest of all the national parks in
the United States is Yellowstone. This park was es-
tablished in 1872. It is in three states--Wyoming,
Idaho and Montana. Yellowstone Park is famous for
its geysers. The most famous geyser is Old Faithful. The park also has boiling pools and hot springs.
One of the finest wild animal preserves in the world
is at Yellowstone.

Grand Canyon National Park is in Arizona. There
is nothing in North America that is more magnificent.
This park is 1009 square miles, which is almost as
large as Rhode Island. At Grand Canyon you will see
what erosion can do. The canyon itself is 200 miles
long and a mile deep.

Yosemite National Park is in the east central part
of California. Here you will see the highest waterfalls
in the world. Some of these waterfalls drop more than
2500 feet. The Yosemite Valley was carved out of the
Sierra Mountains.

Zion National Park was first found by the Mormons.
They were the first white visitors. Here there are.
many unusual rock formations. These rock formations
are of different colored sandstone. Some of them are
red, some yellow, others are brown and gray. The
Mormons gave religious names to these rock formations.
If you go to Zion National Park, be sure to see the
Angel's Landing and the Altar of Sacrifice.

In Bryce Canyon you will also see fantastic rock formations. Bryce Canyon is in Utah. Here there are thousands of different colors in the stone.

Glacier National Park is in Northwest Montana. Some of the most impressive peaks of the Rocky Mountains are in Glacier National Park. It reminds one of the Alps in Switzerland. There are 60 glaciers. There are 250 lakes. There are snow-capped mountains and high waterfalls. The symbol of Glacier National Park is the big horn sheep. These sheep still roam wild on the mountain peaks. The Blackfeet Indians have a reservation just east of the park.

Mount Rainier National Park is in Northwest Washington. This park is one of the finest winter resorts in the United States. For eight months of the year you can enjoy this winter playground. At Mount Rainier National Park it is fun to ski and toboggan.

Sequoia National Park is in California. It is most famous for its trees. Some of these trees are nearly 300 feet high. Some of them are 55 feet in diameter. By the rings on the trees it has been found that they are 5000 years old. They are the oldest and largest of all living things.

Animals

This material is for use around a table, or with four pupils seated in a square. Each pupil has a different sheet. Each pupil reads sentence one on his sheet, person with sheet one beginning. Then each person reads sentence two on each sheet, and so on. The words underscored are the same on each sheet, and in this case give the name of the animal.

Sheet #1   Animals

1. My cat has very long whiskers.
2. The horse was once a very small animal.
3. Our cow gives two quarts of milk every day.
4. A dog is said to be man's best friend.
5. The camel is the ship of the desert.
6. Sheep are supposed to be very stupid animals.
7. The giraffe has a very long neck.
8. A bear loves to eat sweet things.
9. The elephant is supposed to have a very good memory.
10. The mighty lion is the king of the beasts.
11. Monkeys like to swing by their tails.
12. The goat was worshipped as a god in ancient Greece.
13. Our rabbit is white with pink eyes.
14. The beaver builds his home by a stream.
15. Fallow deer run very gracefully.
16. A tiger moves very stealthily.
17. My pig weighs over two hundred pounds.
18. The donkey is sometimes very balky.
19. Fox fur is used to trim women's winter coats.
20. The okapi is a rare animal.

Sheet #2   Animals

1. My cat likes to sit by the fire.
2. The horse was very useful to the pioneer.
3. Our cow is of the Jersey stock.
4. A dog is good company for children.
5. The camel is a very ugly beast.
6. Sheep give us their wool for clothing.
7. The giraffe comes from Africa.
8. A bear sleeps in the wintertime.
9. The elephant sometimes lives to be over 500 years old.
10. The mighty lion is less dangerous than the tiger.
11. Monkeys have very bright little eyes.
12. The goat is supposed to eat tin cans.
13. Our rabbit was caught in the cabbage patch.
14. The beaver has sharp front teeth.
15. Fallow deer are spotted all over their body.
16. A tiger is the most dangerous of all the wild animals.
17. My pig squealed until I gave her some food.
18. The donkey is used for travel in Spain.
19. Fox farms are found in many parts of the East.
20. The okapi lives in the depths of the African forest.

Sheet #3   Animals

1. My cat has a great deal of electricity in her fur.
2. The horse has now been replaced by the machine.
3. Our cow is out in the field of corn.
4. A dog can be trained to do many things.
5. The camel may have either one hump or two humps.
6. Sheep often nibble the grass off down to the roots.
7. The giraffe has short back legs.
8. A bear is one of the most powerful of all animals.
9. The elephant is used for transportation in the Far East.

10. The mighty lion has a thick mane.
11. Monkeys try to imitate people.
12. The goat was milked every morning.
13. Our rabbit has become very tame.
14. The beaver has a fine fur that is used to make hats.
15. Fallow deer have small black feet.
16. A tiger has dark stripes around his body.
17. My pig won two blue ribbons at the county fair.
18. The donkey is sure-footed on the mountain paths.
19. Fox tails are long and bushy.
20. The okapi looks like a zebra and giraffe together.

Sheet #3   Animals

1. My cat is a beautiful Persian.
2. The horse is a popular animal on the race track.
3. Our cow has one brown eye and one black eye.
4. A dog used to be kept at every fire station.
5. The camel has a strange-looking tail.
6. Sheep herding began thousands of years ago.
7. The giraffe eats leaves from the tops of the trees.
8. A bear has heavy padded paws.
9. The elephants at the zoo get a shower bath every afternoon.
10. The mighty lion roared for his mate.
11. Monkeys are very clever thieves.
12. The goat butted the man against the wall.
13. Our rabbit weighs twelve pounds.
14. The beaver destroys many trees.
15. Fallow deer are frightened by the slightest noise.
16. A tiger is the great grandfather of the house cat.
17. My pig was on exhibition at the state fair.
18. The donkey is smaller than the horse.
19. Fox ears are very sharp.
20. The okapi was first heard of in 1901.

Great Bear and Little Bear,

a Greek Myth

(The teacher should have a drawing or picture of the constellations, in order to point out the position of the Great Bear and the Little Bear.)

Callisto was a very beautiful woman. She was admired by the god Jupiter. Jupiter's wife was Juno. Juno was angry because Jupiter admired Callisto. She decided to punish Callisto. She thought and thought and at last she found a way to punish Callisto.

"I will take away her beauty so that no one shall admire her," said Juno.

One morning Callisto was gathering wild flowers in a field. Suddenly she was changed into a bear. Then she fled into a forest nearby. "You shall live in this forest forever! A cave in the rocks shall be your home!" exclaimed Juno.

Although she had the form of a bear, Callisto was still a woman at heart. She was afraid of all the animals she met. She would hide in terror from all the hunters who came into the forest.

One day a young man was hunting in the forest. Callisto saw that it was her son, Arcas. She forgot she had the form of a bear. She rushed toward her son to embrace him. Arcas thought the bear was attacking him. He lifted his hunting spear to kill the bear. Just as he was about to strike, Jupiter appeared. The god snatched away the spear in time to save Callisto's life.

Jupiter took both Callisto and Arcas and placed them in the sky. Callisto became the Great Bear. Arcas became the Little Bear. They have remained in the sky ever since. On clear evenings you can see them in the sky as they move around the North Star.

1. Who was Callisto?
2. By whom was she admired?
3. Who was Jupiter's wife?
4. How did she think out a way to punish Callisto?
5. What was Callisto changed into?
6. Was Callisto changed completely?
7. What did Callisto do when hunters came into the forest?
8. What was the name of Callisto's son?
9. Why did Callisto rush toward Arcas?
10. What did Arcas try to do?
11. Who saved Callisto's life?
12. What did Jupiter do with Callisto and Arcas?
13. Where can you find them today?
14. Do you know any other myths about the stars?

There Still Are Giants

Today we will be talking about the largest living things in the world. Do you know what they are? Some slips have been prepared for pupils to read. We will find out about some giants of today.

1. The largest mammal is the blue whale. The blue whale is sometimes more than 100 feet long. It is the largest mammal that ever lived.

2. The largest animal is the elephant. The elephant is the largest animal alive that lives on land. The African elephant is usually taller than the Asian elephant. The African elephant has very large, floppy ears.

3. The largest reptile is the crocodile. Some crocodiles have been found that were 30 feet long. The salt-water crocodile has a long snout. He is the most vicious man-eater in the world.

4. The largest fish is the whale shark. Some whale sharks grow to be 70 feet long. They have a dark body and round spots all over. The whale shark is a man-eater.

5. The largest flying bird is the wandering albatross. Some of these birds have a wing spread of 11 feet, 4 inches. The albatross has black wings and a white body.

There are some other giant animals in the world today. One of them is the giant tortoise. He lives in the Galapagos Islands. Some tortoises have weighed as much as 593 pounds. Some have measured as much as 8 feet over the shell.

In the Pacific Ocean there lives a giant seahorse. Usually the seahorse is only 3 or 4 inches tall. This giant seahorse is 14 inches tall.

Down in Australia, on the Barrier Reef, grows a giant clam. This clam has a very large shell. Sometimes the shell is more than 36 inches in diameter. If a diver comes close to the clam, he may be caught and may lose his arm or his leg.

There is another giant in Australia. That is the giant earthworm. How would you like to see a fishing worm 12 feet long? These worms burrow in the earth and make very large burrows. If they are caught in the hot sunshine, the worms become dry and brittle. Most of the time they are deep in the mud.

How Naval Vessels Are Named

All ships have names. The Navy gives names to all its vessels. The Navy follows certain rules when it names vessels. Do you know what kinds of vessels there are? There are battleships, there are cruisers, there are gunboats, there are destroyers. There are other kinds of vessels also.

All battleships are named after states. All cruisers are named after cities. The Pittsburgh would be the name of a cruiser. Gunboats are named after smaller cities. Destroyers are named after men who were famous in the Navy.

The minesweeper is a small boat. Minesweepers are named after birds.

Aircraft carriers are usually rather large. They are named for important events in history. They are often named after famous battles. The Yorktown and the Lexington are aircraft carriers.

Submarines became useful in 1911. Submarines had no names. They were just given code numbers like C-4, D-1, K-2. But in 1931 the Navy set up rules for naming submarines. Since 1931 the Navy has named submarines after fishes. All submarines named at the same time received names beginning with the same letter. One group of submarines was named Salmon, Seal, Snapper, and Sturgeon.

What kind of vessels would the following be:

1. Farragut (destroyer)
2. Philadelphia (cruiser)
3. Admiral Dewey
4. Valley Forge
5. Robin
6. Michigan
7. Wichita Falls
8. Barracuda
9. Forrestal
10. California

How Military Officers' Insignia Originated

(Adapted from an article by Lieut. Westerfield in "Read" magazine)

All military officers wear insignia. Have you ever wondered where the idea came from? What was the origin of military insignia? The idea goes back to the 13th century. A great battle had just begun. The lord of the manor had no army. He had to gather together an army to defend his property. So he called all the

men of his manor together. Each man had a definite
responsibility. Each man was given military authority
according to his responsibility.

The private was the man who had one house under
his authority. The first class private wore a chevron.
That was the symbol of the rafter or gables of his one
house. The corporal was in charge of several houses.
He was given two chevrons. The sergeant had a small
village of ten or more houses under his authority. He
wore three chevrons.

The soldier who was in charge of the troops of a
town large enough to have a barricade, wore a bar.
The bar was the symbol of the barricade. This man
was called a lieutenant. The captain came next. He
was given two bars because he commanded a town or
city that was surrounded by a moat.

The major wore an oak leaf. That was because
the major led as many troops as could be seen from
the top of an oak tree.

The colonel wore an eagle. That was because he
commanded as many troops as an eagle could see while
in flight.

The general wore a star because he had as many
troops as could be seen from the stars.

How would you figure out the five-star general?

Letter "W" Game

The teacher gives the sentence. The answer is to be a word starting with the letter "w". This game may be played for team scoring or for individual points.

1. Name something that every husband must have at some time or other.   Wife

2. Name something that always grows faster than the flowers we plant.   Weeds

3. Name something that tells us what time it is.   Watch

4. Name something that we do when we are in church.   Worship

5. Name something that early birds get.   Worm

6. Name something that grows on a sheep.   Wool

7. Name something that Red Riding Hood met in the forest.   Wolf

8. Name something that is used to steer a car.   Wheel

9. Name something that fences are made out of.   Wood or Wire

10. Name something that is the coldest time of the year.   Winter

11. Name something that both a bird and an airplane have.   Wings

12. Name something that the Italians make out of grapes.   Wine

13. Name something that we call a woman who has lost her husband.   Widow

14. Name something that was found in the old-fashioned oil lamps.   Wick

15. Name something that is the home of the President of the United States.   White House

16. Name something that it is not polite to do in company.   Whisper

No Sodas on Sunday

It was the late 19th century. Evanston, Illinois, was a very pious town. It was so pious that a law was passed forbidding the sale of ice cream sodas on Sunday. The town fathers thought this would keep the people away from the soda fountains.

But soon the clerks at the soda fountains thought up something new. They found out how they could obey the law and still serve ice cream. They poured syrup over the ice cream instead of soda.

This soda without soda was what they served every Sunday. After a while, people began to ask for Sunday sodas every day of the week. The town fathers objected again. They said it was wrong to name a dish after the Sabbath day. So the soda fountains changed the spelling of the word Sunday and made it s-u-n-d-a-e-.

26

In that way one of the most popular of all American dishes was begun. Now, who is ready for a chocolate sundae?

Sundae Game

The teacher draws 10 sundae dishes on the blackboard. As she reads the sentences below, whoever understands the flavor mentioned is to come up, give the sentence to the class and then initial his sundae dish. Whoever gets the most "sundaes" wins the game.

1. I would like a strawberry sundae.

2. May I have a butterscotch sundae?

3. Will you have a marshmallow sundae?

4. I believe I'll have a chocolate sundae.

5. That peanut sundae looks good to me.

6. Let's have a hot fudge sundae.

7. I'm going to have a pineapple sundae for dessert.

8. I paid 40¢ for a walnut sundae.

9. My brother always orders a peach sundae.

10. I can never tell the difference between a caramel and a butterscotch sundae.

The Origin of the Menu

(Adapted from "Facts and Fancies" by Bombaugh)

When you go to a restaurant, you are usually given a menu. From the menu, you choose the food that you want. Sometimes there are many different items on the menu. It would take a long time for the waitress to tell you all the different items. The menu helps to save time when you order a meal.

Do you know where the idea of the menu began? It began in a city called Regensburg in Germany. In the year 1489 there was a meeting of the Electors. The host for the meeting was the Elector Henry. He gave a state dinner. Every time before he ordered a dish, he referred to a long piece of paper. One of the men who sat near him asked the Elector Henry what he was reading. The Elector did not say a word. He gave the long paper to the other gentleman.

On the paper was a list of all the food that had been prepared for the dinner. The Elector had asked the cook to make up this list for him.

Everyone at the meeting heard about the paper. The idea of having such a list pleased everyone. When the men went to their homes they brought the idea back with them. Each man introduced the menu to his own family. In this way, the idea of the menu was spread all over the world.

Ordering From the Menu

The teacher prepares slips; each student gets up before the class and reads his slip.

1. I will have fruit cocktail, fried shrimp, French fried potatoes and a cup of coffee.

2. I will have a bowl of vegetable soup, some roast beef and mashed potatoes, and a pot of hot tea.

3. I will have a shrimp cocktail, scalloped oysters, lettuce with French dressing, and a piece of apple pie.

4. I will have a ham sandwich, some potato chips and a small coke.

5. I will have two scrambled eggs some bacon, four slices of toast and a cup of coffee.

6. I will have tomato juice, Virginia baked ham, sweet potatoes, salad, corn muffins and coffee.

7. I will have a salad bowl with Russian dressing, some whole wheat bread, a glass of milk and some chocolate ice cream.

8. I will have some beef stew, a glass of milk and some cherry pie with ice cream.

9. I will have some orange juice, toast and two fried eggs.

10. I will have some fried chicken, a baked potato, asparagus and some jello with whipped cream.

Tall Tale

Every year the Liars Club of America has a convention. The stories told at this convention are always without a word of truth. However, this tall tale that we are going to tell seems to have a basis of fact. Does it seem foolish to you?

Once there was a little Indian boy named Hiawatha. He had a rainbow trout for a pet. Hiawatha named the trout Butch and kept it in a barrel.

The trout became larger and larger. Hiawatha had to change the water every day. This was a lot of trouble. Then he decided that he would teach Butch to live out of water.

First, he began by taking Butch out of the water for just a minute or so, and then he kept it out longer each time. Pretty soon, the trout could stay out of the water for some time, if it was in the wet grass.

After a while, it didn't even matter if the grass was wet or not. Butch could live in the shade. By then the fish had become so tame that it followed Hiawatha like a dog. And in a short while, when it didn't need water at all any more. the trout followed Hiawatha everywhere.

One morning Hiawatha started off for town. Butch wiggled after him. On the way, they came to a bridge. Hiawatha noticed that a board was out. There was a hole in the bridge. But he didn't bother about that.

A little while later, Hiawatha turned around and Butch wasn't there. So Hiawatha ran back, looking

high and low for his fish. Pretty soon, he came to
the hole in the bridge again. He looked down the hole
and there he saw Butch. He was floating on the water.
with his belly up.

The poor trout had fallen in the water and drown-
ed---because he had forgotten how to swim.

   1.   What was the little Indian boy's name?
   2.   What kind of pet did Hiawatha have?
   3.   What did Hiawatha call the trout?
   4.   Where did he keep Butch?
   5.   What did Hiawatha decide he would do?
   6.   How did Hiawatha train Butch to stay out of
      water?
   7.   After a while, how tame did Butch become?
   8.   Where did Hiawatha go one morning?
   9.   What did Hiawatha notice when he crossed
      the bridge?
 10.   When did Hiawatha miss the fish?
 11.   Where did he find the trout?
 12.   What had happened to the trout?

PUERTO RICO

(Adapted from an article in "The Prudential" magazine)

If so desired, the teacher may prepare slips of
paper and have the pupils read the sentences.

1. Puerto Rico means "rich port."

2. Puerto Rico is an island.

3. The island of Puerto Rico was given to the United States after the Spanish-American War.

4. Puerto Rico is three times as large as Rhode Island.

5. But Texas is 77 times as large as Puerto Rico.

6. Most of the people in Puerto Rico speak the Spanish language.

7. Puerto Rico was discovered by Christopher Columbus.

8. Columbus discovered Puerto Rico on his second trip to America in 1493.

9. The capital of Puerto Rico is San Juan.

10. The city of San Juan was founded in 1511 by Ponce de Leon.

11. Ponce de Leon was once the governor of Puerto Rico.

12. Ponce de Leon is buried in the Cathedral of San Juan.

13. There is a wall all around the city of San Juan.

14. It is one of the finest examples of an old walled city.

15. How would you like to take a trip to Puerto Rico?

The Apple Tree Game

The teacher draws an apple tree on the blackboard. Twenty circles for apples are drawn on the tree. The teacher reads the sentences. Each time a pupil understands a sentence correctly he may put his initials in an apple. The object of the game is to see who "gathers" the most apples.

1. An apple a day keeps the doctor away.

2. The boy gave his teacher a round, red apple.

3. These apples were sent from the state of Washington.

4. Would you like to peel some apples for me?

5. Mother is making some applesauce for lunch.

6. Did you ever bake an apple pie?

7. Put the apple blossoms in the vase on the table.

8. I'd like to have some ice cream on my apple pie.

9. We sat in the shade of the old apple tree.

10. The golden apple was given as a prize for beauty.

11. The child was the apple of her father's eye.

12. The baby's cheeks were as red as an apple.

13. How much did you pay for the basket of apples?

14. The apple orchard is a beautiful sight in the spring.

15. Some bad boys shook all the apples off my
neighbor's tree.

16. Don't forget to wash the apple before you eat it.

17. Johnny Appleseed brought apple trees to the
Ohio Valley.

18. The apple is shiny because there is wax in the
skin.

19. The robins have a nest in the top of the apple
tree.

20. All the apples that fell from the trees were used
to make cider or vinegar.

The Story of Johnny Appleseed

(Adapted from "The Hurricane's Children" by
Carl Carmer)

This is the story of how Johnny Appleseed brought
appleblossoms to the West.

Johnny Appleseed was born in Boston. Massachusetts
He was born in 1775. His real name was Jonathan
Chapman. When he was a baby, the first thing he saw
was the appleblossoms outside the window. He always
liked appleblossoms after that.

When he was nineteen years old, he built himself a house in Pittsburgh. There he planted a big apple orchard. There were a lot of bees in the apple orchard. They made a great deal of honey. Johnny gave the honey to his neighbors. He never charged them anything for the honey. He said the bees made it for him for nothing.

Jonathan Chapman lived in Pittsburgh for twelve years. For twelve years he had one idea growing in his head. He wanted to take a load of appleseeds to the pioneers in the West. He wanted them to have apple orchards and appleblossoms, too.

In the year 1806, Jonathan Chapman filled two canoes with appleseeds. He started down the Ohio River. He travelled many miles down the river until all the seeds were given away.

The farmers began to talk about this strange fellow. They called him Johnny Appleseed.

Johnny went back to Pennsylvania. He went to the cider mills and got more seeds. He was a strange-looking fellow. He had blue eyes, long hair that came to his shoulders, and he always went barefooted.

When Johnny came back to Pennsylvania the third time, he was still more changed. His clothes were very ragged. He wore a coffee sack, with holes in it for arms and legs. For a cap he wore a tin kettle in which he also cooked his food.

Strange stories began to come out of the West.

A trapper had once found Johnny Appleseed playing with three bear cubs while the mother bear watched fondly. Johnny Appleseed knew directions so well he never used a compass. He did not feel the cold of winter. He could walk barefooted in below-zero weather without freezing his toes.

One time, Johnny Appleseed heard that some of his friends were going to be attacked by the Indians. He ran through a forest for sixty miles and saved the lives of the people living in the fort.

The state of Ohio became beautiful with pink apple-blossoms. The banks of the Wabash River were planted in apple trees. The farmers everywhere welcomed Johnny Appleseed.

One day Johnny walked twenty miles to reach the home of a friend who lived in Indiana. He sat down on the doorstep to eat his evening meal. It was bread and milk as usual. He read aloud from the Bible for a while. Then he stretched out on the floor and went to sleep. He never woke up from that sleep.

Today we know how far Johnny Appleseed went. There are a hundred thousand square miles of apple orchards and appleblossoms from Pennsylvania to the middle West.

The Bell of Atri

This is an old story. It is a story about justice.

In the city of Atri in Italy there lived a prince. The prince wanted all his people to be happy. He knew that to be happy they must have justice. He wanted all his people to be just and fair. He had a large bell hung in the market place. It became famous as the bell of justice. Whenever a wrong was done, the person who felt wronged rang the bell. Then the prince or a counsellor came to hear the story and to give justice.

The bell was rung many times. Rich and poor, old and young were given justice. As the years went by, so many people rang the bell that the bell rope wore off. Someone fastened a piece of grapevine to what was left of the rope.

One afternoon as all the people were taking their afternoon nap, the bell began to ring. The people wondered who was ringing the bell. They wondered who had been wronged. They rushed to the market place. There they saw an old horse. He was lame and thin and looked as if he were starving. The horse was chewing on the leaves of the grapevine because he was so hungry. In this way, he had rung the bell of Atri.

When the prince arrived at the market place he tried to find out who was the owner of the horse. It was found that the horse belonged to a soldier. The horse had carried his master through many battles. Now he was old and of no value to the soldier. He had been turned out on the road to shift for himself.

The prince was very angry. He saw that the soldier had been unjust to the old horse. The prince said that the horse had rung the bell of Atri and justice would be given to him. The soldier was ordered to appear before the prince. The prince told the soldier he would have to build a fine barn for the horse. He also ordered the soldier to feed the horse on the finest grain for the rest of his life. In this way justice was given because the bell of Atri had been rung again.

1. Where was the city of Atri?
2. What did the prince want for his people?
3. Why did the prince have the bell in the market place?
4. After many years, what happened to the bell rope?
5. How was the bell rope repaired?
6. Who rang the bell one afternoon?
7. How had the horse rung the bell?
8. What did the prince do when he arrived at the market place?
9. To whom had the old horse belonged?
10. What did the prince order the soldier to do?

One Little Grain of Mustard Seed

Once there was a little girl who took an umbrella
to church with her and it brought about a miracle. It
happened in a farming country. There was a terrible
drought. For many weeks there had been no rain.
Unless it rained very soon, the crops would all be lost.

So the minister sent word for everybody to come
to church the next Sunday. Everybody was going to
pray for rain.

When Sunday came, it was very hot. The sun
was shining brightly and not a cloud was in the sky.
The farmers came driving down the roads to church.
The townspeople came walking to church.

Every pew was filled. Then the minister read
to them from the Bible. He read about all the many
beautiful miracles, and then the people prayed. People
who had never prayed before cried out, "Let us have
rain, O God, let us have rain!"

And after a while, the church began to grow dark.
Then the sound of thunder was heard. And finally there
came the loveliest sound of all. All the people heard
the sound of rain on the roof. The skies opened and
drenched the world. It rained and rained and rained.

But nobody could go home from church because
nobody had brought an umbrella! That is--no one
except one little girl. She had brought her umbrella
because she was sure if she prayed hard enough it
would certainly rain. And there she stood. She was
the one little grain of mustard seed in the midst of
unbelief.

The Umbrella

(Adapted from "I Wonder How" by Milton Goldsmith)

Do you know who was the first person to have an umbrella? It was probably the cave man. He probably used a big palm leaf. A little while later, he tied together a number of palm leaves. This made a very fine shade from the hot sun.

The word umbrella is a Latin word. It comes from "umbro" which means "shade." People did not think of using umbrellas in the rain.

The umbrella had a religious meaning. In ancient Egypt, no religious festival could be held unless an umbrella was carried over the priest's head. In the old Hindu temples, the pictures show the people with umbrellas over their heads.

The umbrella was also a sign of nobility. Even today, in Siam, a very large umbrella is always carried over the head of the King when he goes out. In India, the rulers of various provinces have a special title. It is, "Lord of a hundred umbrellas." That means the ruler has so many provinces under him.

Even today the umbrella is still used in religious ceremonies. The coverings over the thrones of bishops are really large umbrellas. The cardinals also have the privilege of umbrellas over their heads in any religious procession.

Umbrellas were not used for the rain until the 15th century. The French and the Italians were the first to do this. But the common people never had umbrellas. Only the rich and noble people had umbrellas.

In the 18th century there were many coffee houses in England. It became the custom for each coffee house to have a large umbrella. This was for travellers who were caught in the rain.

The man who made the umbrella popular was an Englishman. His name was Jonas Hanway. He had lived in the Orient for a while. When he came back to London, he always carried a big green heavy cloth umbrella. He never forgot his umbrella. It was always under his arm, rain or shine. People laughed at him. After a while they saw how wise he was. Then other people followed his example.

Umbrellas at that time were very big and heavy. The ribs were made of whalebone. How many ribs do our umbrellas have now? In the early 1900's, some umbrellas had 40 ribs.

Today, our umbrellas are usually made of plastic or of a waterproof fabric. They are light and easy to carry. Some are even small enough to fold into a small package. You may buy an umbrella that you can see through. But they still have not made an umbrella that you won't forget!

Did you ever leave your umbrella in a bus or street car? The transit companies say they find more umbrellas than anything else!

Musical Heroines

In each song mentioned, a girl is involved. Can you name the girl?

1. Is there anyone finer, in the state of Carolina?

   Dinah

2. In all my dreams, your fair face beams.

   Adeline

3. And when the fields are fresh and green, I'll take you to your home again.

   Kathleen

4. Light she was and like a fairy, though her shoes were number nine.

   Clementine

5. You'll look sweet upon the seat of a bicycle built for two.

   Daisy

6. I've come from Alabama with my banjo on my knee; I'm going to Louisiana my true love for to see.

   Susanna

The Common Pin

(Adapted from the "Mueller Record, " May 1939)

The common pin is a very useful object.

The first pin was probably a thorn. In the Stone Age, pins were made of bone. Around 2000 B. C., pins made of bronze were used. By the 14th century, the finest pins were made of brass. Some were made of iron wire. These were against the law of the time, because pins were supposed to be manufactured only from brass.

Pins could be sold only on the first and second day of January. Women would save their money all year so they could buy their supply of pins on these two days. The money they saved was called "pin money." This expression has come down to us today.

Most of the pins of the 15th century came from France. Then England began to manufacture pins. By the year 1636, London had a corporation or guild of pin manufacturers. The city of Birmingham became famous for its pins.

Pins were made in the United States as early as 1775. The city of Birmingham in Connecticut began to manufacture pins in 1836. Today, the state of Connecticut is still the largest producer of pins in the United States.

There are many different sizes of the common pin. The largest is the $3\frac{1}{2}$ inch blanket pin. The smallest is a very fine, gilt pin used by entomologists. These pins are so small that 4500 of them weigh only one ounce.

How Fashions Start

(Adapted trom ''American Digest,'' January 1941)

Some fashions are very strange. Some fashions in women's clothes have no rhyme or reason. Some fashions begin through accidents. It was an accident that gave us the fashion for wearing very small hats. Women still wear small hats perched on their heads. This fashion began in the late 1870's.

The Countess de Castiglione was said to be the lovliest woman of the Second Empire. She had been on a court picnic. Everyone was having a wonderful time at the picnic. The Countess was having such a good time that she forgot all about her little dog. The Countess had left her broad-brimmed hat on the grass. The little dog amused himself by chewing away the brim of the Countess' hat. All that was left was the little felt crown with its trimming of roses.

The Countess laughed when she saw what her little dog had done. She said she would wear the little hat back to Paris. She perched the hat on the front of her head. She looked very beautiful in the little hat. Everyone who saw the Countess in her hat wanted a small hat just like it. In a few days all the smartest women in Paris were wearing small brimless hats.

Do you see how a fashion can start?

A Geography Game

Today some excellent jigsaw puzzle maps of the United States can be purchased. Get one that is so made that each state can be taken out as a separate piece. The teacher can ask the questions and the pupil who knows the correct answer will take out the state named. The winner is the one who has the greatest number of states.

Here are some sample questions.

1. What state is famous for its peach trees?
   Georgia

2. What state is famous for its production of movies?
   California

3. What state is famous for its potatoes?
   Idaho

4. What state is famous for its great Salt Lake?
   Utah

5. What state is famous for its thoroughbred horses?
   Kentucky

6. What state is the largest of all the United States?
   Alaska

7. What state is the smallest of all the states?
   Rhode Island

8. What state is famous for the largest and tallest buildings?

   New York

9. What state is famous for its oil wells?

Oklahoma

10. What state is famous for its production of automobiles?

Michigan

11. What state is famous for its mules?

Missouri

12. What state is famous for its cheese and other dairy products?

Wisconsin

13. What state is famous for its tobacco?

Virginia or
Connecticut

14. What state is famous for its tall corn?

Iowa

15. What state is famous for its wheat fields?

Kansas

16. In what state will you find the Liberty Bell?

Pennsylvania

17. In what state will you find Old Faithful geyser?

Wyoming

18. In what state will you find flamingos and alligators?

Florida

19. What state is famous for its shrimp?

Louisiana

20. In what state will you find Harvard University?

Massachusetts

Carillons

(Adapted from "The Book of Bells" by Satis Coleman)

{ It would be well for the teacher to have pictures of
each of the bell towers mentioned. }

A carillon is a group of bells. There must be at
least four bells in a carillon. There are two very famous carillons in America. Of course there are many
other carillons. But these two are the most famous.
One is in the Riverside Church in New York City. The
other is in the Bird Sanctuary in Florida.

The largest carillon in the world is in Riverside
Church. It hangs in the bell tower there. It was given
by John D. Rockefeller, Junior. He gave it in memory
of his mother. The bells were hung in 1930. They are
in the belfry of the tower, which is 400 feet high.

This carillon has 72 bells. The bells were made
in England. The largest bell weighs twenty tons. The
smallest bell weighs only ten pounds. Four bells of
this carillon play chimes every day. They play chimes
for fifteen minutes three times every day. The tune
they play is from an opera, "Parsifal". There are
also concerts given several times a· week from this
carillon.

The second largest carillon in America is at
Mountain Lake in Florida. This carillon was given to
the people of the United States by Edward Bok. It is
often called the "Singing Tower". The "Singing Tower"
was built in 1929. It is 205 feet high.

This carillon has 61 bells. They were also made in England. In front of the tower is a beautiful lake. It is a reflection pool. All around the lake are trees and bushes. Here there are birds of all kinds. When the carillon plays, the birds sing, too. The music carries for many miles because the Singing Tower is at the highest point in the state of Florida.

1. What is a carillon?
2. Where is the largest carillon in the world?
3. Who gave the carillon to the Riverside Church?
4. Where were the bells for this carillon made?
5. Are the bells played very often?
6. Where is the second largest carillon in America?
7. Who gave this carillon to the people of the United States?
8. What is the tower often called?
9. Describe the surroundings of the "Singing Tower".
10. Why does the music from this carillon carry for many miles?

Travel Through Space

The teacher will prepare 16 slips of paper with the following sentences. Each pupil will get up before the class and read the sentence he has "pulled." The sentences are to be read in order. They may also be used for four people as table practice material. For the latter, pupil #1 has sentences 1, 5, 9 and 13; pupil #2 has sentences 2, 6, 10 and 14; etc.

1. I have just read a story about an imaginary trip to Venus.

2. It no longer seems strange to talk about visiting the other planets.

3. You would have to travel to Venus in a special space ship.

4. Such a ship would probably use atomic power.

5. It would have to be of special construction to keep from burning up.

6. The space ship might start its trip from a satellite station orbiting the earth.

7. The trip to Venus would probably take around 145 days.

8. The days on Venus are much longer than the days on earth.

9. The climate is much warmer, too.

10. A trip to Mars would be farther than a trip to Venus.

11. It would be just as simple to visit Mars as to visit Venus.

12. Mars has four seasons, but they are nearly twice as long as ours.

13. A year on Mars lasts 687 days, but a year on Venus is only 225 days.

14. Would you rather spend a year on Venus or a year on Mars?

15. I prefer to remain on the familiar planet, Earth.

16. I'm afraid space travel is not for me.

"Con" Words

The teacher reads a sentence. The members of the class have slips bearing the second sentence which contains a word beginning with "con." The pupils come up and read their sentences before the class.

1. Are you happy where you live now?
   I am perfectly <u>content</u>.

2. I hope all of you have faith in me.
   We have the utmost <u>confidence</u> in you.

3. How many vowels are there in this word?
   There are not as many vowels as <u>consonants</u>.

4. My brother is reading a serial story in that
   magazine.

   It always says "To be continued" at the most
   thrilling part.

5. The small boy tried to hide his embarassment.
   He never was able to conceal his feelings.

6. Do you think she is telling the truth?
   I can confirm everything she has said.

7. That man is now a Doctor of Philosophy.
   Who conferred the degree upon him?

8. This is evaporated milk.
   My husband prefers condensed milk.

9. Are you going abroad this summer?
   I hope to spend two months travelling on the
   Continent.

10. This bird house was built by a Boy Scout.
    It's a fine piece of construction.

11. Do you understand the meaning of this word?
    I am not familiar with the connotation.

12. I just spoke to my brother on the telephone.
    Did you limit your conversation to five minutes?

13. I cannot remember the author of "Green Pastures."
    Wasn't the author Marc Connally?

14. This chest is a very old piece of furniture.
    It was built shortly after the conquest of Mexico.

15. What kind of automobile are you planning to buy?
    I'd like to buy a convertible.

It's All in the Point of View

This was one of President Franklin Roosevelt's favorite stories:

A man down in Atlanta, Georgia owned a farm. He did not live on the farm, but had a tenant farmer. He took four friends with him to visit the farm.

When the visitors came into the tenant farmer's house, they were a little embarrassed. The farmer had only two chairs. So the visitors stood around for a few moments.

Then the owner of the farm said to the tenant farmer, "I don't believe you have enough chairs here. "

The old farmer glanced around at the group. Then he muttered, "I have plenty of chairs. I just have too much company. "

1. Where did the owner of the farm come from?
2. Whom did he have living on his farm?
3. How many friends did he take with him to visit the farm?
4. How did the friends feel when they entered the farmhouse?
5. How many chairs did the farmer have?
6. What did the owner of the farm say to the farmer?
7. How did the farmer feel about that?

That's How It Started

(Adapted from the "Reader's Digest")

In 1896, a young man was working in a factory. There was much heavy machinery there. This machinery shook the whole building. The young man was not very well. The jarring of the machinery bothered him very much. But he could not afford to leave his job. So he made up his mind to do something about his problem.

One morning he brought a rubber mat to the factory. He stood on this rubber mat. At once he found relief. The jarring of the machinery did not annoy him when he stood on the mat.

But after several days, someone stole this mat. So he bought two small pieces of rubber. He fastened them on to the heels of his shoes with small nails. This idea gave him two rubber mats that nobody could steal.

The name of that young man was O'Sullivan. He was the inventor of rubber heels. Today his firm is very large. It is one of the largest manufacturers of rubber heels in the world.

Politeness

A small boy was visiting at a neighbor's house. He stayed at the neighbor's house for dinner. When he came home his mother asked him about his manners at the table.

"Were you perfectly polite?" she asked.

"Well," said the little boy, "When I was trying to cut my meat it slipped off on the floor. But I was real polite about it."

"What did you do, dear?" asked his mother.

"Oh," said the little boy, "I just said very carelessly, 'That's always the way with tough meat!'"

Bananas

(Adapted from "Mueller Record," March 1940)

Do you like bananas? At first, people did not like bananas. It took a long time before this strange fruit became popular. People had to learn to eat it.

A long time ago there were no bananas in the United States. They were first imported into the United States in 1869. The first bananas were brought to New Orleans from the Spanish Honduras. In 1870, a few bunches were brought to New York City from Panama. Today, most of the bananas are imported from Jamaica or Martinique.

The original home of the banana is doubtful. It is supposed to have come from the East Indies. Now it grows in almost every tropical and subtropical country in the world.

In tropical countries, the banana is a very important food. The ripe bananas are used to make flour. This flour is used to make bread and cakes.

Sometimes one tree will produce as much as 56 pounds of bananas. These bananas are picked before they are ripe. They are picked from the tree while they are green. Then they ripen on the voyage to the United States.

1. Where was the original home of the banana?
2. Where can the banana be grown today?
3. Why are most of the bananas picked before they are ripe?
4. From where are most of our bananas imported?
5. What is the value of the banana as a food?

Where Would You Be ?

1. Where would you be if you were watching a picador?

   Mexico or Spain

2. Where would you be if you were in the Mammoth Cave?

   Kentucky

3. Where would you be if you were on the slopes of Mt. Everest?

Himalaya Mountains

4. Where would you be if you were on the Great White Way?

Broadway, New York

5. Where would you be if you were touching the Liberty Bell?

Philadelphia

6. Where would you be if you were in the Sugar Bowl?

New Orleans

7. Where would you be if you were on Flirtation Walk?

West Point

8. Where would you be if you lived in a sampan?

China

9. Where would you be if you were in the Louvre?

Paris

10. Where would you be if you were in the ruins of the Coliseum?

Rome

Watch Out !

In this game, the teacher reads the sentence and the pupils guess what part of a watch is described.

Find the following things on your watch:

1. This is something that you use to look into the future.

   ### Crystal

2. This is something that you also find on a flower.
   ### Stem

3. This is something that is found under the mattress of a bed.

   ### Springs

4. This is something that the secretary always reads at the beginning of a meeting.
   ### Minutes

5. This is something that we use in mathematics.
   ### Figures

6. This is something that everyone has, even new babies.

   ### Hands and Face

7. This is something that a lawyer always likes to have.

   ### Case

8. This is something that in football language is some-
    times full, sometimes half, sometimes quarter.

    <u>Back</u>

9. This is something the little boy always likes to
    have when there is ice cream for dessert.

    <u>Seconds</u>

She Got It In

A little girl had received a wristwatch for a birthday present. For days she could talk about nothing else.
No matter what the subject of conversation was, she
always managed to draw attention to her watch.

One evening, the minister came to dinner. The
little girl's father had told her if she mentioned the
watch just once she would be sent upstairs and to bed.
The whole family was surprised when the little girl never said a word about her watch.

After they all sat down at the dinner table, the
minister said to the little girl, "I hear you always say
grace at the table. Would you like to recite a Bible
verse for grace this evening?"

The little girl nodded her head. Then with a spar-
kle in her eye, she said in a very loud voice, "What
I say unto you now, I say unto you always, <u>watch</u>!"

Something About Flowers

(The teacher should try to have pictures of the flowers named and should write the names on the blackboard.)

These are some of the flowers that we shall talk about:

tulip	sunflower	nasturtium
crocus	violet	lily
dandelion	thistle	rose
poppy	poinsettia	iris

Flowers were grown in very early times. We are not sure where the first gardens were planted. In Africa, the Pharoahs of Egypt had beautiful gardens. In America, the Aztecs had many bright flowers in their palaces.

The first tulips grew wild in Persia. Their name comes from a Persian word that means turban. Around

1550, some tulips were brought to Vienna. They were brought from Turkey by the Austrian Ambassador. From there, they were planted all over Europe. Early in the 17th Century, the Dutch people became known as the greatest growers of tulips. Rare bulbs were auctioned for thousands of dollars. Today the Dutch people are still famous for their beautiful tulips.

In 1531 the Spanish conquistadors came to Peru. They found that the Incas worshipped the sunflower. In 1615, the Indians of the Georgian Bay section in Canada were using the sunflower as a food.

The nasturtium came from Peru or the West Indies. Sir Walter Raleigh was supposed to have brought the plant to England from the West Indies. The pirates loved to eat the leaves of the nasturtium. In the 16th Century the leaves were often used in salads. At that time the flowers were very small. There were not so many different colors of flowers. The nasturtiums were then yellow with red spots.

The name of the crocus comes from the Greek language. The Greeks and the Arabs called this flower saffron. The first home of the crocus was in Asia Minor. The juice of the crocus was used to make dye and medicine. For a long time no crocus bulbs were allowed to get outside the country of Kashmir. Then, in the 14th century a pilgrim from England brought a crocus root back to England. There he planted the root. The crocus bloomed and spread all over the country.

In the Middle Ages, people were very fond of violets. They used them for food. The people chopped up violets, onions and lettuce for a salad. Sometimes they cooked a violet broth. The violet was the favorite flower of Napoleon. When Napoleon was exiled he told his friends he would come back when the violets bloomed again. From the time he left France until he returned in 1815, the violet was the secret badge of his followers.

The lily was also used as a food. The lily grew wild in China and Tibet. The people used to eat the lily bulbs just as we eat potatoes. The Calla Lily came from Africa. It grew near the Cape of Good Hope.

The dandelion blooms almost anywhere. The name of the flower comes from a French word. The word means lion's tooth. The French people gave it that name because the jagged leaf looks like the teeth of a lion. The Swiss people call the dandelion another name. They call it Shepherd's Clock. That is because it opens at five o'clock in the morning and closes at eight o'clock in the evening.

Do you know why the thistle is the emblem of Scotland? In the year 1263 there was a war between the Scots and the Danes. The Danes were planning a surprise attack. They stole upon the Scots' camp very quietly. All their men were barefooted. All at once there was a loud cry. One of the barefooted Danes had stepped on a thistle. The Scots were warned just in time and were able to defeat their enemy. After that time the thistle became the symbol of the Scots.

There are many stories about the rose. It was said that Cleopatra covered her banquet floor with 18 inches of rose petals. Cleopatra also had her mattress stuffed with these petals. The rose is the national flower of England. The Chinese people serve rose fritters on New Year's Day.

The poppy is a native of California. When the Spaniards were exploring the west coast of North America, they found the coast covered with the California poppy. The Spaniards thought the flower was sacred.

The poinsettia grew wild in tropical North America. It was named after Joel Poinsett of Charleston. He was the first United States Minister to Mexico. He brought the flower with him and persuaded his friends to cultivate it. The poinsettia became one of the symbols of the Christmas season.

There are more than 170 different kinds of iris. The word comes from the Greek. It means rainbow. The Greeks probably called it iris because it is found in many different colors. Another name for the iris is a French word. It is called fleur-de-lis. Louis VII was King of France. He was going to the Holy Land. That was in the year 1137. His soldiers carried a white banner. The day Louis VII started on his journey, the white banner was covered with purple flowers. The king felt this was a symbol. He used the purple iris as the emblem of France. The soldiers called the flower a fleur-de-Louis. Later this name became fleur-de-lis. It is still the symbol of the French.

Do you know what flowers are called the flowers of the month? Here they are:

January	carnation	July	water lily
February	primrose	August	poppy
March	violet	September . .	dahlia
April	lily	October . . .	begonia
May	lily-of-the-valley	November . .	chrysanthemum
June	rose	December . .	poinsettia

The Story of the Common Eel

(Adapted from "Fishes" by Bertha Morris Parker, Basic Science Education Series, Row, Peterson and Co. (now Harper & Row Publishers, Inc.)

Have you ever seen an eel? The eel is a very common fish. This story is about the life of an eel.

The story starts in the middle of the Atlantic Ocean. Here is where the eggs of the eel are found. These eggs were floating in the water. The water was very, very salty. The water was also very cool. The water was deep in this part of the ocean, and it was very dark.

One day something happened. An egg hatched. The little eel that came out of the egg didn't look like an eel at all. He was flat as a piece of paper. You could see right through him. He looked as if he were made of glass. He was about two and a half inches long. He had a small head but his teeth were long.

There were millions of other eels who hatched about the same time. Do you know what baby eels are called? They are called elvers. All of these elvers started to swim around in the water. The elvers had no large eels with them. There was no one to teach them what to do. They started to swim nearer and nearer to the top of the water.

By the time they had come near the surface of the water, the eels were ready to start on a long trip. Some of the eels swam toward America. Some of the eels swam toward Europe. Here is a very strange thing. How did the eels know which way to swim? It has been found that the difference between the

American eel and the European eel is in the number of vertebrae. If a baby eel had more than 111 vertebrae, it would swim toward Europe. If the baby eel had less than 111 vertebrae, it would swim toward America.

The eel in our story swam toward America. He swam for many months. When he was about a year old, the eel reached the shores of the United States. Then he swam and swam until he came to a large river. All this time, the eel had many other eels with him. But the other eels became fewer and fewer. They were swallowed by the big fish. Our eel was very lucky. He escaped from all these big fish.

Our eel was beginning to change his shape. He wasn't flat any more. Now he was becoming round like a worm. He had lost his teeth. He was beginning to develop fins. But you could still see through him.

The eel began to swim up the river. He traveled for more than two hundred miles up the river. Then he came to a branch of the river. The eel swam for many, many miles until he came to a smaller branch of the river. Now the water was not salty. It was fresh water. But the eel had changed, so the fresh water did not bother him. He was growing darker. His body was growing longer and longer. He was becoming fatter and rounder. His fins were well developed.

One day the eel swam into a small lake. Here he stayed for some time. The eel ate and ate and ate. He ate everything he could find. Sometimes he ate worms; sometimes he ate fish. Sometimes he ate small shellfish. Sometimes he buried himself in the mud and went looking for food only at night.

The eel lived in the lake for many years. He became very bold. He wasn't afraid of anything. Many fishermen tried to catch him, but he was lucky. He was never caught. The eel would have made a fine meal, because now he was very large. He was about 36 inches long. His body was smooth and firm.

When the eel was about eight years old, a strange thing happened. It was at the end of the month of August. The eel left the lake. Some of the other eels also left the lake. They all started back toward the place where they had been hatched. Our eel was a female eel. It was going back to lay its eggs in the same place where it had been hatched.

The eel swam and swam. It swam for more than a thousand miles. Then, at last, the eel and its companions reached the part of the ocean where they had first lived.

The eel went down deep into the water. It swam to where the water was very dark and cold and salty. Here the eel laid its eggs. The eel laid more than five million eggs. And after the eggs were laid, the mother eel soon died. But the eggs were there in the ocean. Perhaps, after a while, one of those eggs hatched and followed the same path as the eel of our story.

How Many Birds Are in Your Tree ?

(The sentence material has been adapted from "Birds"
by Bertha Morris Parker, Basic Science Education
Series, Row, Peterson and Co. (now Harper & Row,
Publishers, Inc.)

For this game the teacher prepares trees cut out
of green cardboard or heavy paper. Each pupil is
given a tree. There are to be twelve slits in the top
part of the tree. The teacher then reads the sentences.
Whoever understands the sentence comes up, repeats
it to the class, and then receives a small bird which
the teacher has cut out of paper and colored. The
pupil puts one bird in each slit in his tree. The pupil
who collects the most birds in his tree wins the game.

1. All birds are animals.

2. All birds are warm-blooded.

3. Birds are the only animals that have feathers.

4. There are many different bird families.

5. All birds come from eggs.

6. Different kinds of birds build different kinds of nests.

7. The baby birds must have a great deal of food.

8. Birds have different kinds of bills.

9. The song sparrow has a short, heavy bill.

10. The hummingbird has a long, slender bill.

11. The owl has a strong, curved bill.

12. Different kinds of birds are fitted for eating different kinds of food.

13. Some birds help us by eating harmful insects.

14. Some birds help us by eating the seeds of weeds.

15. Some birds help us by eating mice.

16. Almost all birds have some kind of song.

17. Most birds help us much more than they harm us.

18. There are birds in almost every part of the world.

The Owl

(Adapted from an article by Wm. Bridges in "Good Housekeeping")

We often think of the owl as a wise old bird. But owls are just like human beings. Some are wise and some are foolish. There are about two hundred kinds of owls in the world. There are about 18 or 20 different kinds of owls in the United States.

Some owls have a very long life. There is a kind of owl in northern Asia that has lived to be over 65 years old.

Owls are of all shapes and sizes. The biggest owls are 2 1/2 feet long. The smallest owls are only as large as a sparrow. The female owls are usually larger than the males. The owl's feathers are very heavy. Many owls have feathers even on their toes. When an owl flies, he makes very little noise. Owls are the most silent of birds when they fly. Their wing feathers have soft filaments. These filaments muffle sound.

Some owls sleep at night and hunt for food in the daytime. Most of the owls hunt for their food at night. Do you believe an owl cannot see in the daytime? All owls can see in the daylight. When it is dark, owls depend a great deal on their sense of hearing. They use their ears as much as their eyes.

The owl has no feathered friends. Everybody fights with him. Owls even enjoy fighting with each other. Most owls avoid human beings. The owls will attack people if they come near the owl's nest when the baby owls are in the nest.

Owls have their nests almost anywhere. They nest in holes in the ground, in hollow trees, in old wells, or in church steeples. Some owls build their nests in barns. Other owls take over the old nests of other birds or of squirrels. The owls are not fussy about how they build their nests. They just throw together a jumble of leaves, moss, or sticks, whatever they can find.

One Barn Owl was not a very wise owl. She laid 24 eggs. She laid them on a bare tin roof. There was no nest and no shade. Every one of the eggs was cooked!

Owls are of great value to man. The farmer feels the owl is his best friend. The owls eat up rats and mice. In 1890 to 1892 there was a plague of field mice. This was in southern Scotland. The mice overran the farms. The whole area might have been destroyed by the mice. But owls began to gather there. Little by little the owls ate up all the mice and saved the farmers' crops.

There was an owl in New England who was very smart. He used to perch in a certain tree every evening. Every evening a woman used to put some pies outside to cool. The pies were on the steps of the back porch. The owl would wait until the woman went back into the house. Then he would swoop down from the tree. But he never touched the pies. He would grab the mice that crept out to nibble the pies.

We like the story about another wise owl. One owl was trying to impress a female. He was fluffing out his feathers. Then he would flap his wings and snap his bill. But the female was not impressed. Then the male owl saw a rabbit. He swooped down and grabbed the rabbit. Then he dropped the rabbit at the female's feet. That impressed her. They ate the rabbit side by side. The male began his courtship dance. The female joined in. She probably thought she had found a good provider. Wasn't she a wise owl?

How People Were Given Their Names

Today, most people have three names. A long time ago, each person was called by only one name. In ancient times a person was named according to some personal characteristic. Or the name might have related to some fact about the person's birth. We read stories in the Bible about Abraham, Isaac and Jacob. Abraham meant the father of a multitude. The name Isaac meant laughter in the Hebrew language. The boy was given that name because there was much laughter and rejoicing when he was born. Not everybody was given a brand-new name. Some people were named after famous forefathers. But there were no family names.

A Roman had three names. The Romans started the custom of giving more than one name to a person. The first name was a personal name; the second name was a clan name; the third name was a family name. One famous Roman was named Gaius Julius Caesar. The first name meant "joyous." The second name meant he belonged to the clan of Julia. The third name meant he came from the Caesar family.

In ancient England, family names were given to avoid confusion. Too many people had the same first name. Family names were often taken from the person's occupation, or their home country or from their nicknames. James, who was a cook by trade, was called James Cook. Thomas, who came from Scotland, was called Thomas Scott. John, who was strong and powerful, was called John Strong.

By the middle of the 14th century, most people in England used more than one name. This custom has come down to the present day.

Do you know where your name came from? Do you know what your name means? Here are a few of the meanings of some common given names:

Charles comes from the Teutonic language. It
        means of great strength.
Philip comes from the Greek language. It means
        lover of horses.
Paul also comes from the Greek language. It
        means small or gentle.
Ruth comes from the Hebrew language. It means
        a vision of beauty.
Mabel comes from the Latin language. It means
        beloved or beautiful.

When Were You Born ?

(Adapted from "Astrology--Your Place in the Sun"
by Evangeline Adams)

{ It is a good idea to have flash cards with the Zodiac }
{ signs on them. }

Do you believe in astrology? Do you know what astrology is? Astrology is called a false science. It is claimed that it tells about the influence of the stars and the planets on people. Each person is said to be born under a certain sign. The signs of the Zodiac are said to rule one's life. There are twelve signs of the Zodiac. These are the signs: There is Aries, the Ram. There is Taurus, the Bull.. There is Gemini, the Twins. There is Cancer, the Crab. There is Leo, the Lion. There is Virgo, the Virgin. There is Libra, the Scales. There is Scorpio, the Scorpion. There is Sagittarius, the Centaur. There is Capricorn, the Goat. There is Aquarius, the Man pouring water. There is Pisces, the Fishes.

If you were born between January 21 and February 20, you were born under the sign of Aquarius. A person born at this time is always a little ahead of other people. He is very optimistic. He rarely quarrels with anyone. This person has very good common sense. He loves to share his knowledge with others. He is the best domestic type.

If you were born between February 20 and March 22, you were born under the sign of Pisces. You would be careless with money. You would be extremely sensitive. This person is a wanderer, never wanting to stay in one place very long. Often, this person has a poor business sense. He is always open to suggestion, and sees everything through rose-colored glasses.

If you were born from March 22 to April 21, you are under the sign of Aries. This person is a pioneer. He always has a lot of initiative. He is also impulsive. A person born under this sign is extremely honest in all money matters.

If you were born from April 21 to May 22, you are under the sign of Taurus. You are inclined to be slow, lazy, patient, and calm. This person is extremely warm-hearted. He is fond of home life. His mind is often in his muscles.

If you were born between May 22 and June 22, you are under the sign of Gemini. You would have a pretty good time out of life. A woman under this sign is often a flirt. This person tries to walk in two directions at once. He is not reliable when it comes to money matters.

If you were born between June 22 and July 24, you are under the sign of Cancer. You would take things as they come. You would often overlook some of the practical things in life and favor the more romantic things. This person has a love of travel. He would also make a good teacher or guide.

If you were born between July 24 and August 24, you are under the sign of Leo. You would be a born leader. You would be very generous with money. This person likes to exaggerate. He is a hard worker and never bears a grudge against anyone. He has great faith in other people.

If you were born between August 24 and September 24, you are under the sign of Virgo. You would be a thrifty person. You would enjoy driving a good bargain. This person has a lot of patience and foresight. He is also extremely practical.

If you were born between September 24 and October 24, you are under the sign of Libra. You would be very persuasive. You would always think things out carefully. This person is devoted to beauty. He is always plausible.

If you were born between October 24 and November 23, you are under the sign of Scorpio. You would never beat around the bush. You would be a fine organizer. You would have a lot of personal magnetism. You would also be rather selfish. A person born under this sign makes a very good surgeon.

If you were born between November 23 and December 23, you are under the sign of Sagittarius. You would be extremely logical. You would be very much interested in the outdoor life. You would be impatient. Many times, this person makes promises and then forgets all about them. This person also has a high strung temperament.

If you were born between December 23 and January 21, you are under the sign of Capricorn. You would be "penny-wise and pound-foolish". You would have a lot of patience. You would take life as a serious thing. This person has a conservative mind. He also has a great capacity for work.

A Sign of the Zodiac

The teacher will ask the question. The pupil who knows the answer writes it horizontally in the blocks provided. When complete, the blocks outlined will reveal a sign of the Zodiac.

2		C	O	L	U	M	B	U	S
4		P	A	C	I	F	I	C	
7			A	P	P	L	E		
1			A	P	R	I	L		
9		O	S	T	R	I	C	H	
5			C	H	U	R	C	H	
3				B	O	S	T	O	N
8		C	A	L	E	N	D	A	R
6					C	O	C	O	O	N

1. What is the fourth month of the year?

2. Who discovered America in 1492?

3. Where is the capital of the state of Massachusetts?

4. Which ocean is the largest, the Atlantic or the Pacific ?

5. Where do many people go on a Sunday morning?

6. What does a moth spin before it becomes a butterfly?

7. What fruit did Eve give Adam in the Garden of Eden?

8. What do we have on the wall or the desk to tell us the months and the days of the year?

9. What is one of the largest birds that do not fly?

The Christmas Question

The teacher draws squares and the numbers on the blackboard (or on separate sheets of paper) as in the following illustration. Horizontally, the squares should spell the last word in the sentence the teacher reads. The first vertical spaces in each group should be specially outlined, for at the completion of all the squares the question will then stand out. The students must watch for the last word in each sentence. After writing the word in the proper squares, the student gives the entire sentence to the class.

1 i c e
2 s h o p

8   t r e e
17 h o m e
3   e a c h
13 r i d e
9   e d g e

7 a n g e l

14 s m i l e
4   a p p l e
10 n a m e s
5   t a k e n
18 a c t o r

6   c o m e
15 l a m b
11 a r m s
16 u p o n
12 s t a r

?

1. The streets were covered with snow and <u>ice</u>.

2. You will find some lovely dolls in the toy <u>shop</u>.

3. Those books are twenty-five cents <u>each</u>.

4. Would you rather have an orange or an <u>apple</u>?

5. Where did you have your picture <u>taken</u>?

6. Do you think she will <u>come</u>?

7. I wish I had wings like an <u>angel</u>.

8. Are you going to have lights on your Christmas <u>tree</u>?

9. The pie was dark brown all around the <u>edge</u>.

10. How do you remember all their <u>names</u>?

11. The woman had a small baby in her <u>arms</u>.

12. The Wise Men followed the <u>star</u>.

13. I have a new car; will you come along for a <u>ride</u>?

14. Her face was bright with a lovely <u>smile</u>.

15. Would you rather have beefsteak or <u>lamb</u>?

16. I feel as if I were being spied <u>upon</u>.

17. What time are you going <u>home</u>?

18. That man (substitute current favorites) is a fine <u>actor</u>.

Now, what is the great Christmas question?

What I Want in My Christmas Stocking

The teacher types sentences on twelve slips of paper and has the pupils draw for them. Each pupil reads, in order, the sentence he has chosen.

1. I want a new wristwatch in my Christmas stocking.

2. I want a baby brother in my Christmas stocking.

3. I want a new Ford car in my Christmas stocking.

4. I want some expensive perfume in my Christmas stocking.

5. I want a pair of woolen mittens in my Christmas stocking.

6. I want a permanent wave in my Christmas stocking.

7. I want some brotherly love in my Christmas stocking.

8. I want a subscription to "Life" magazine in my Christmas stocking.

9. I want a diamond ring in my Christmas stocking.

10. I want a rich husband in my Christmas stocking.

11. I want a trip around the world in my Christmas stocking.

12. I want some peace on earth, good will toward men in my Christmas stocking.

The Christmas Seal Angel

Every year there are different designs for the Christmas seal. In 1939 the Christmas seal had an angel on it. The seal was designed by Rockwell Kent.

A certain woman wrote a letter to Rockwell Kent about the seal. She wrote, "Is that supposed to be an angel on the Christmas seal? It doesn' t look much like an angel to me."

Rockwell Kent wrote a letter in reply to the woman. He said, "My dear madam, how do you know what an angel should look like? Have you ever <u>seen</u> an angel?"

1. What kind of design did the Christmas seal have in 1939?
2. Who was the designer of the seal?
3. What did a certain woman do?
4. What did she write in the letter?
5. Did Rockwell Kent reply?
6. What did he say in his letter?

A Christmas Quiz

1. At what point of the compass, north, south, east or west, was the Christmas star?

<u>East</u>

2. What animals did the Three Wise Men use to travel to Bethlehem?

<u>Camels</u>

3. Where was there no room for Mary and Joseph?

Inn

4. How many reindeer does Santa Claus have?

Eight

5. What do the French children put out for their gifts instead of hanging up stockings?

Wooden Shoes

6. Give some other names by which children around the world call Santa Claus?

Kris Kringle
St. Nicholas
Pere Noel, etc.

7. Who wrote the story about the Cratchits and Tiny Tim?

Dickens

8. What is the real name of the poem which begins, " 'Twas the night before Christmas and all through the house--"?

A Visit From
St. Nicholas

9. Who wrote this poem?

Clement Moore

10. Give the names of the Three Wise Men.

Caspar, Melchior
and Balthasar

11. Name three plants we think of in connection with Christmas.

Poinsettia, Mistletoe
Holly

12. Who were in the fields watching their flocks by night ?

Shepherds

13. What gifts did the Three Wise Men bring ?

Gold, Frankincense, Myrrh

14. What is another name for a Christmas song or hymn ?

Carol

15. What character in a Mother Goose rhyme was eating a Christmas pie ?

Jack Horner

16. What are the Christmas colors ?

Red and Green

Her First Turkey

A bride of a few months had just prepared her first Christmas turkey. She brought it into the dining room on a large platter. She was very proud of the turkey.

"There you are," she told her husband. "There is my first roast turkey!"

"It's wonderful!" said the husband. "How beautifully you have stuffed it, too!"

"But I didn't stuff it," cried the bride. "This turkey wasn't hollow."

About St. Patrick

St. Patrick's Day occurs on the 17th of March.
There was a dispute in Ireland about the date of St.
Patrick's birth.   Some people said it was on the eighth.
Other people said it was on the ninth.   To settle the
dispute, the two dates were added together.   This made
his birthday the 17th of March.

Patrick was born at Dumbarton in Scotland around
396 A. D.   When he was sixteen years old, he was
captured by pirates.   They took him to Ireland where
he became a slave.   He stayed in Ireland for six long
years.   During that time he learned to speak the Irish
language. Finally he escaped from Ireland and after
many difficulties came back to Scotland.   But he was
not in Scotland very long before he had a strange dream.
This dream told him that the Irish people wanted to
have him teach them.   He believed this dream should
be followed.

Patrick went to France.   He studied for fourteen
years so he could be a missionary to Ireland.   When
he went to Ireland, he was made a Bishop.   People say
that when St. Patrick came to Ireland there were no
Christians; but before he died there were no more
heathens.

St. Patrick did a great deal to make the Irish people
a Christian people.   He wanted them to realize that
there is a great "Three in One. "   So he took a shamrock
leaf and told the people that just as three leaves are
fastened to one stem, so are there three persons in
one God.   Since that time, the shamrock has been the
national flower of Ireland.

Do you know the story about how St. Patrick drove all the snakes and vermin out of Ireland?

Do you know why we wear green on St. Patrick's Day?

"Green" Words Game

Each sentence below contains a "green" word. The teacher reads the sentence. Whoever understands the entire sentence writes the green word on the blackboard and receives a green paper shamrock from the teacher. The pupil who collects the most shamrocks wins.

1. Will you please mow the grass for me?

2. That flower has a heart-shaped leaf.

3. The emerald is the birthstone for May.

4. The watermelons are ripe in July.

5. The boys caught a grasshopper and brought it to school.

6. Would you like to have a tomato and cucumber salad?

7. I'm going to have some spinach for supper.

8. The old bullfrog was croaking in the pond.

9. Will you pay back that five-dollar bill you owe me?

10. Will you sell me a <u>one-cent stamp</u>?

11. There was a tall <u>pine tree</u> at the top of the hill.

12. The <u>eyes of the cat</u> were shining in the dark.

13. The <u>stems</u> of the roses were very long.

14. The rocks on the north side of the hill were covered with <u>moss</u>.

Columbus Day Quiz

1. Why do we celebrate October 12 as Columbus Day?
<u>On that day he sighted land</u>
<u>of new world</u>

2. What is the day of Columbus' birth?
<u>Unknown, year 1451</u>

3. Give the names of the three ships Columbus used to cross the ocean.
<u>Nina, Pinta, Santa Maria</u>

4. How many voyages of discovery did Columbus make? <u>Four</u>

5. For what country did Columbus claim America?
<u>Spain</u>

6. Who were the rulers of Spain when Columbus sailed for the New World?
<u>King Ferdinand and Queen</u>
<u>Isabella</u>

7. In what year did Columbus discover America?
   <u>1492</u>

8. Give the names of two islands which were also discovered and named by Christopher Columbus.
   <u>Haiti, Trinidad, Jamaica</u>

9. After whom was the New World named?
   <u>Americus Vespucius</u>

10. In what city was Columbus born?
    <u>Genoà, Italy</u>

11. What did Columbus want to prove about the world?
    <u>That it was round</u>

12. Columbus had a son. What was his name?
    <u>Diego</u>

Pumpkin Race

The teacher should have orange pumpkins cut out of heavy paper. Each time a pupil understands a sentence and can repeat it to the class, he receives a pumpkin. Object of the race is to see who can collect the most pumpkins.

1. The pumpkin grows in a field.

2. The frost is on the pumpkin.

3. There are beautiful flowers on the pumpkin vine.

4. Can you bake a pumpkin pie?

5. We always have pumpkin pie for Thanksgiving dinner.

6. The pumpkin is a symbol of Hallowe'en.

7. How much does that pumpkin weigh?

8. Will you carve a funny face on your pumpkin?

9. Put the pumpkin in the window on Hallowe'en.

10. What shall we do with the pumpkin seeds?

11. We can string the pumpkin seeds for a necklace.

12. The Indians were the first people to plant pumpkins.

13. Many people eat the dried pumpkin seeds just as we eat almonds.

14. Of what value are pumpkins to man?

Easter Game

The teacher reads the sentence. The pupil who gets the entire sentence writes only the last word on the blackboard. The word should be capitalized. Each word is to be directly beneath the previous word, with a double space after the fifth.

1. At Easter time, many of the boys and girls who are away at college or school, come Home.

2. Some of them come home by train, others come home by Automobile.

3. Would you rather go to Virginia or Pennsylvania?

4. My father will have to stay home and work as usual at the Pentagon.

5. At Easter time, the daffodils are beautiful and Yellow.

6. The rabbit brings children many colored Eggs.

7. Some of these eggs are works of Art.

8. Everyone is happy because it is Spring.

9. I am going to buy my mother a pot of red Tulips.

10. I would like to buy lilies, but they are too Expensive.

11. I am going to give my little brother a big chocolate Rabbit.

May Words

The teacher prepares slips with the following sentences. The pupils read the sentences they have drawn and the class members find the word that has the "may" sound in it.

1. My girl friend's name is <u>Mabel</u>.

2. The captain and the first <u>mate</u> stayed with the ship until it went down.

3. What was your mother's <u>maiden</u> name?

4. This beautiful linen tablecloth was <u>made</u> in Ireland.

5. My grandmother always put cinnamon and <u>mace</u> in her pumpkin pies.

6. The Three Wise Men were called the <u>Magi</u>.

7. A wrestling match will be the <u>main</u> event of the show.

8. I sent you the books by third class <u>mail</u>.

9. Did you ever spend your summer vacation on the coast of <u>Maine</u>?

10. You will have to <u>make</u> some excuse for me.

11. Her grandfather was a <u>major</u> in the first World War.

12. Do you still <u>maintain</u> that you are right?

13. That woman uses too much <u>makeup</u> on her face.

14. The lion's _mane_ was filled with burrs.

15. Where is the _Malay_ Peninsula?

16. Who is the _Mayor_ of New York City?

17. I like to hear a _male_ quartet sing "Sweet Adeline."

18. Did your ancestors come to America in 1620 on the _Mayflower_?

19. Will you have oil or _mayonnaise_ on your salad?

20. My sister was the _matron_ of honor at her friend's wedding.

21. There was so much confusion I felt as if I were in a _maze_.

22. The month of _May_ was named after the mother of Mercury.

Common Cold

(Adapted from the "Readers Digest," Feb. 1948)

One evening Mr. Smith went into a restaurant. He had a very bad cold. He was sniffling all the time. The waiter knew Mr. Smith very well. The waiter said, "What's the matter, Mr. Smith? Are you fighting a cold?"

"Yes," said Mr. Smith. "I have an awful cold."

The waiter shook his head very sadly. "It's too bad that you don't have pneumonia," he said. "They know what to do for that."

1. Where did Mr. Smith go one evening?
2. What was the matter with Mr. Smith?
3. How well did the waiter know Mr. Smith?
4. What did the waiter ask Mr. Smith?
5. How did Mr. Smith reply?
6. What did the waiter think about that?

You're as Old as You Feel

A young woman sat down beside an old man in the lobby of a hotel. The old man started a conversation with her.

"I feel like I was 75 years old this morning," said the old man.

"Oh, that's too bad," replied the young woman.

"No, that's wonderful," said the old gentleman. "Because I'm 85 years old today."

1. Where did the young woman sit down?
2. Who started the conversation?

3. How old did the old man feel?
4. What reply did the young woman make?
5. Did the old gentleman feel the same way about it?
6. Why did feeling 75 seem wonderful to him?

In a Jam

One afternoon, Mrs. Brown called her little boy into the kitchen.

"Johnny," she said, "would you like to have some strawberry jam?"

"You bet I would, Mother," said Johnny.

"Well," said Mrs. Brown, "I was going to give you some to put on your bread, but I've lost the key to the pantry."

"Don't worry, Mother," said Johnny, "You don't need a key. I can reach down through the window and open the door from the inside."

"That's just what I wanted to find out," said Mrs. Brown. "I knew someone was stealing the jam and I had to make sure it was you."

The Secret

An old gentleman had reached the age of 101. A newspaper reporter came to interview him. He asked the old man how he had been able to live to such a ripe old age.

The old man said, "I never smoked, I never drank, I never overate. I was in bed by ten o'clock every night and up at six every morning."

The reporter looked doubtful. "Why, I had an uncle who did the same thing, but he died when he was 71."

The old gentleman replied very calmly, "The trouble with your uncle was, he didn't keep it up long enough."

Trying to Be Alone

Once upon a time there was a man who wanted to live all by himself. He wanted to live a very simple life. So he gave up his job, left behind all the things he owned, and went to live in the forest.

He built himself a cabin with only one room. The weather was always warm, so he wore very few clothes. But unfortunately, there were mice in the forest. The mice came into the cabin and bothered him very much. The mice bothered him so much that he had to keep a cat to catch the mice.

The cat had to have milk to drink, so he had to buy a cow. There had to be somebody to take care of the cow. So he hired a boy. Then the man had to build a house for the boy to live in.

The man also had to hire a woman to care for the house and make meals for the boy. It was very lonely in the forest for the woman, so the man built a few more houses. He invited some of the woman's friends to come and live in the new houses. In this way, after a while there came to be a whole new town.

Then the man found out he could not live all by himself. He said, "The farther we seek to go from the world and its cares, the more they multiply."

She Had a Good Job

A father and mother had three small children. One day the mother left the children alone. They were alone all day. The father came home at five o'clock. He asked the children if they had been good children.

"Oh, yes," said his small daughter, "we were all very good. I washed the lunch dishes."

"And I wiped them dry," said his small son.

The father turned to the baby of the family. "Well, Margaret," said the father, "what did you do?"

The little girl was very happy to give her reply. In a loud voice she announced, "I picked up the pieces."

Silver and Selfishness

Do you know what a parable is? It's a story that teaches a lesson. See if you can find the moral lesson in this story.

One day a very rich old man was visited by a priest. The rich man was also a very selfish man. He never gave help to anyone.

The priest took the rich man by the hand and led him to a window.

"Look out there," said the priest. So the rich man looked out into the street.

"What do you see?" asked the priest.

"I see men, women, and little children," answered the rich man.

Then the priest took the rich man by the hand again and this time he led him to a mirror on the wall.

"What do you see now?" asked the priest.

"Now I see myself," replied the rich man.

Then the priest said: "In the window there is glass, and in the mirror there is glass. But the glass of the mirror is covered with a little silver. As soon as the silver is added, you no longer see others, but you see only yourself."

Full House

A middle-aged woman met a bride of a few weeks. The bride and her husband had just moved into their new home.

"How are you getting along with your new eight-room house?" asked the woman.

"Oh, not so bad," replied the bride. We have completely furnished one of the bedrooms by saving soap coupons."

"But why don't you furnish the other seven rooms?"

"We can't," said the bride. "They're full of soap."

1. Who met a bride of a few weeks?
2. Who had just moved into a new home?
3. What did the woman ask the bride?
4. What room had the bride and her husband furnished?
5. What had they saved in order to buy the furnishings?
6. What did the woman want to know about the other rooms?
7. Why couldn't the other rooms be furnished?

Eternity to Pay

An American had just arrived in Heaven. St. Peter met him at the pearly gates. He showed him all around and then gave him a beautiful harp.

"Here is your golden harp," said St. Peter.

The newly-arrived American looked at the harp, then at St. Peter.

"I knew there must be a catch in this," he said. "How much is the first down payment?"

Cause For Divorce

A man was asking the court for a divorce. The judge
asked him why he wanted a divorce from his wife. The
man replied, "Judge, that woman is always asking me
for money. When I come home from work at night, she
asks me for money. Money, money -- all the time she
does nothing but ask me for money."

"But Mr. Brown," said the judge, "what does she do
with all that money?"

"Oh, I don't know," answered Mr. Brown. "I never
gave her any."

In Chicago They Would

A girl from Chicago was spending some time on a
farm in the South. She and the farmer were walking
through a pasture where there were a lot of cows. The
girl spoke to the farmer about the troubled way in
which the cattle seemed to look at her.

"Well," said the farmer, "it must be on account of
that red dress you are wearing."

"My goodness!" said the Chicago girl, "Of course
I know the dress is out of style, but I had no idea a cow
would notice that."

Vermont Rocks

A man from New York City was visiting in Vermont.
He was staying with a Vermont farmer. He said to the
farmer, "There are so many rocks here. Where did
they come from? Do you grow rocks in Vermont?"

The farmer replied, "Those rocks were brought

here by the great glacier."

The man from New York asked, "What became of the glacier?"

"Oh," said the farmer, "The glacier went back north to get more rocks."

Abandoned to His Fate

Farmer Jones was sitting with his wife behind a palm tree on a terrace of a Florida hotel. A young man and his girl friend sat down on a bench near them. The young man began to tell the girl how beautiful he thought she was. He told her how much he loved her and how much he thought of her.

Behind the palm tree, Mrs. Jones whispered to her husband, "Oh, John, he doesn't know we're here. I believe he's going to propose to her. Whistle to warn him."

"What for?" asked Jones, "Nobody whistled to warn me!"

Good Sleeping Quarters

Billy was four years old. He was visiting his grandmother. One morning the grandmother asked Billy to help her get the family down for breakfast. She promised Billy five cents if he would get his Uncle John out of bed.

Billy went upstairs, very sure of himself. In a few minutes he was downstairs again. His grandmother said, "I'll give you your five cents now, if Uncle John is out of bed."

"I didn't get him up," said Billy. "He gave me twenty-five cents to let him alone."

They Couldn't Sleep

Two brothers were sleeping in the same bed. They had to share a room because some relatives had arrived unexpectedly for the weekend.

In the morning, around seven o'clock, one brother said, "Hey, Bill, did you get much sleep last night?"

"No, I couldn't sleep a wink all night," complained Bill.

"Neither could I," said his brother. "I heard every sound and every noise all night long."

Then they pulled their heads out from under the bedcovers. They saw that the bed was covered with plaster. The ceiling had fallen on them during the night----- and they hadn't even noticed it.

Alarmed

A shopper came into a department store. She said to the clerk, "I want to buy an alarm clock. But I don't want just any old thing. I want one that will wake up my husband without waking the whole family."

"I'm very sorry, madam," said the clerk, "we don't have that kind. All we have is the ordinary kind. They wake up the whole family without disturbing father."

Successful

Two women were talking about how they felt. One woman said, "I always feel better after a good cry."

"Oh, is that so?" said the other woman. "I suppose that's because it gets things out of your system."

"Oh, no," said the first woman, "but it gets things out of my husband."

Education Comes High

An Englishman was talking to an American friend. "How is it that most Americans get along well in business, while so many Englishmen fail?"

"It's a matter of brains," was the reply. "You should eat more fish. Fish is the thing to give you brains. I'll tell you what we'll do. You give me five dollars. I'll buy you the same kind of fish my wife buys for me. Then, you eat some and see if you don't become smarter."

The Englishman gave the American five dollars. The fish was sent to him. The following week the Englishman met the American again.

"How did you like the fish?" asked the American.

"Oh," said the Englishman, "it was splendid fish!"

"Do you feel any different now?" asked the American.

"No, I can't say that I feel any different," said the Englishman. "But five dollars was a lot to pay for that small piece of fish, wasn't it?"

"There you are!" cried the American. "Your brain is beginning to work already!"

How Right!

A man had been going out with a young woman for ten years. He called on her regularly every Wednesday and Saturday evening.

His friends asked him, "You've been courting that girl for ten years; why don't you marry her?"

The young man replied, "If I married her I wouldn't have any place to go on Wednesday and Saturday evening."

A Bouncing Baby Boy

A father, a mother, and a baby kangaroo were out
for a walk.   After a while, the baby kangaroo became
tired and crawled into his mother's pouch. All was
fine for a while. Then the baby began to jump out of
the mother's pouch, only to crawl back in again. The
father kangaroo became angry at the baby because he
had been in and out of the pouch at least seven or eight
times. Then the mother kangaroo solved the mystery.
"Don't scold the baby, " she said. "He can't help it.
I have the hiccups. "

Making Matches

A teacher was asking her class some questions.
"Jimmy, can you tell me how matches are made?"
she asked.
"No, ma'am," replied Jimmy, "but I don't blame
you for asking. "
"What do you mean by that?" asked the teacher.
"Well, " said Jimmy, "my mother says you've been
trying to make a match for 20 years. "

He Would, Too

A very beautiful young woman was a model in New
York City. She went for a trip to Paris. One day she
was walking down the avenue all by herself. All at once
she felt that someone was following her. She stopped by
a shop window and saw a young man behind her. She
walked on for several blocks and the young man kept
following her. He began to compliment her. The young
woman became angrier and angrier. After four blocks

she saw a traffic policeman. She rushed up to the policeman and said, "Officer, that man back there has been following me for several blocks!"

The policeman looked at the man. Then he looked over the beautiful young woman. He took off his cap, made a sweeping bow and said, "My dear young lady, if I were not on traffic duty I would follow you too!"

He Was a Provider

Bessie was the new maid at the Smith's home. One morning Mrs. Smith was talking to Bessie about her family. She asked, "Bessie, do you have a husband and family?"

"I have no family, but I have a husband," replied Bessie.

Mrs. Smith wondered whether Bessie's husband was good to her, so she asked, "Bessie, is your husband a good provider?"

Bessie laughed out loud. "Yes, ma'am," she answered, "He sure is a good provider. He's just about the best provider I know about. He's going to buy me some furniture, providing he gets a house. He's going to buy me a house, providing he gets a job. He's going to get a job, providing the work isn't too hard. Yes, ma'am, that husband of mine is just about the best provider that ever was."

Getting There

The operator of an elevator in a large apartment building seemed very happy one morning. He was laughing and singing to himself.

"You must be very happy this morning," remarked a passenger.

"No, sir," said the operator. "I am not very happy this morning. I'm just trying to get happy."

Running Away From Home

Little Johnny was four years old. One day he told his mother that he didn't like his home any more. So his mother told him that if he didn't like his home he could pack up his clothes and leave.

Johnny thought it over. Then he gathered a few things together and left the house.

Half an hour later, a neighbor woman saw little Johnny. He was walking up and down the street. He was carrying his small suitcase. The neighbor woman asked him, "Where are you going, Johnny?"

Johnny replied, "Oh, I'm running away from home."

"Well," said the woman, "You will never get anywhere by just walking up and down the sidewalk."

"I know it," said Johnny, "but I'm not allowed to cross the street."

1. Who was the boy in the story?
2. How old was Johnny?
3. What did he tell his mother about his home?
4. What did his mother tell him to do?
5. How did Johnny feel about that?
6. Who saw little Johnny about a half hour later?
7. What was Johnny doing?
8. What did he have in his hands?
9. Where did Johnny say he was going?
10. What did the neighbor woman say then?
11. Why was Johnny staying on the sidewalk?
12. Do you believe Johnny thought more of his home after that?

That's French Politeness

(Adapted from "A Speech and Story for Every Occasion"
by B. F. Thomas)

Billy had been away to a private school. He came home for spring vacation. His father was very happy to have him at home.

"I'm glad to see you at home again, Billy," said the father. "How are you getting along at school?"

"Fine!" said Billy. "I've learned to say 'thank you' and 'if you please' in French.

"Why, that's marvelous!" exclaimed the father. "That's more than you ever learned to say in English."

Blame It on the Teeth

An old minister had once given very fine sermons. But now he wouldn't preach any more because he had no teeth.

The members of his congregation wanted to do something for him. They took up a collection and decided to buy him a pair of false teeth. They sent an order to Sears, Roebuck & Company for a set of teeth, both uppers and lowers.

A few weeks later the teeth arrived. They were a perfect fit and the old minister was very much pleased.

So, he began to preach sermons again. The first Sunday he preached for a half hour, as usual. The next Sunday he preached for an hour. On the third Sunday he preached for one hour and a half. Each Sunday the sermons became longer and longer.

Finally, the members of the congregation said they couldn't stand it any more. They would have to do something about the situation. They blamed everything on the teeth. So they wrote a letter to Sears, Roebuck & Company and explained the whole situation.

Several days later, a letter arrived from Sears, Roebuck & Company. They said they were very sorry. They must have sent the old man the wrong set of teeth. The teeth that he had received were <u>women's</u> teeth.

Sounding Off

A new pulpit had just been put up in a church. The minister and the janitor were trying out the acoustics.

"Now stand far in the back of the church and tell me how this sounds," said the minister, and he repeated a few words of the Twenty-Third Psalm.

"That's fine, pastor; that's fine," said the janitor.

"Now you go up in the pulpit and say anything you like," suggested the minister.

The janitor walked slowly up into the pulpit. He thought for a moment, then he said, "I haven't had a raise in pay for three years. How does that sound, pastor?"

1. What had just been put in a church?
2. Why were the minister and janitor there?
3. Where did the minister ask the janitor to listen to him?
4. What did the minister repeat?
5. How did that sound to the janitor?
6. What did the minister suggest?
7. Did the janitor have anything to say?
8. Do you believe the minister could understand that?

He Was Tidy

(Adapted from "Boys' Life," Nov. 1940)

A mother had been teaching her little boy to be tidy. She talked to him all the time about being tidy. She impressed on him the fact that he must be tidy at all times.

One afternoon they were going for a bus ride. Before they got on the bus, the mother gave the little boy an orange. They got on the bus before the little boy could eat the orange. The mother told the little boy he could eat the orange on the bus, but he would have to be very tidy about it.

Then the mother saw a friend of hers. They started a long conversation. The mother forgot all about the little boy. When it was time to get off the bus, the mother looked around for the boy. The two of them got off the bus in a hurry.

When they had gotten off the bus, the mother said to the little boy, "You were a very tidy boy. You didn't throw your orange peels on the floor of the bus." Then the mother had a strange look on her face.

"By the way," she said, "Where did you put the orange peels?"

"Oh," said the little boy, "I didn't want to throw the peels on the floor. I wanted to be tidy. So I put the orange peels in the pocket of the man who sat next to me."

Word For Word

Mark Twain went to hear a sermon one Sunday morning. It was a very fine sermon. After it was over, Mark Twain spoke to the minister of the church.

"I certainly enjoyed your sermon this morning," said Mark Twain. "I welcomed it as I would welcome an old friend. I have a book at home in my library that contains every word of that sermon."

"Why, that's impossible," said the minister.

"No, sir," said Mark Twain, "It's absolutely so."

"Well," said the minister, "I would certainly like to see that book."

"All right," replied Mark Twain, "you shall have it."

The next morning the minister received a book in the mail. It had been sent with the compliments of Mark Twain. It was a dictionary.

Weather Report

A politician was feeling sick. He asked his wife to take his temperature. She went to the cabinet in the bathroom and brought out the first instrument she laid her hands on. There were several thermometers and barometers around the house. It just happened that the instrument she put her hands on was a barometer. By mistake she put the thing into the politician's mouth. When she took it out, the politician said, "What does it read?"

"It must be right," she said as she shook her head. "It reads 'dry and windy.'"

The Indian Chief and the Businessman

An American businessman was traveling through the west. He noticed an Indian chief peacefully smoking in front of his wigwam.

"Chief," said the businessman, "why don't you get a job?"

"Why?" grunted the chief.

"Well," said the businessman, "then you could earn a lot of money."

"Why?" insisted the chief.

"Because if you earned a lot of money you could always save some and have a big bank account."

"Why?" again asked the chief.

"For heaven's sake!" shouted the businessman, "with a big bank account you could retire. Then you wouldn't have to work any more."

"I'm not working now," pointed out the chief.

He Got What He Asked For

One November, during the hunting season, a man became lost. He couldn't find the other members of his hunting party. He walked for miles and the farther he walked the darker it became. Finally he came to a farmhouse. He was cold and hungry. It was a raw night and the family had already gone to bed.

The hunter pounded on the door. No one came. He pounded again. This time a window was raised on the second floor. A man's voice asked, "What do you want?"

"I want to stay here all night," shouted the hunter.

"All right; stay there," replied the farmer, and he slammed the window down.

Hanging On

The lights had suddenly gone out in a bus. A tall man asked the woman who had just got on if he could help her to find a strap.

"Oh, I've already found a strap, thank you," she said.

"Well, then," suggested the man, "would you mind letting go of my necktie?"

Artistic Finish

An artist thought he would like to paint his studio. He wanted to give a new finish to the walls. So he gave them a coat of shellac. Then he waited for the walls to dry. Every day he examined the walls. Every day they seemed as wet and as sticky as when the shellac was first put on.

The artist was puzzled. He thought it must have been a very poor quality of shellac.

A few days later his wife solved the mystery. She came rushing into the studio from the kitchen.

"Where is that big can of maple syrup I had in the basement?" she asked.

Then the artist knew what was the matter. He had shellacked the walls of his studio with maple syrup!

Fair Criticism

The Brown family had just come home from church. They were all sitting at the dinner table. Then Father Brown began to criticize the sermon. He said the minister spoke too fast. Then Mother Brown criticized the music the organist played. Ruth and Barbara thought the choir was all out of tune.

But little Billy Brown was very thoughtful. He finally announced, "I think it was a pretty good show for my five cents."

Probably Not

A rather stout schoolteacher was talking to her class about birds. She was telling them about different birds and their habits. The class talked about robins, sparrows, bluejays and wrens.

Then the teacher said, "I have a canary at home in a cage. That canary can do something that I could never do. Who can tell me what it is?"

One small boy raised his hand and said, "I know, teacher. The canary can take a bath in a saucer."

Roughage

(Adapted from "Scholastic" magazine, March 25, 1940)

An American family moved to a foreign country. They were afraid that they wouldn't be able to get some American foods. They were also afraid they wouldn't like foreign cooking. So they took with them a supply of all kinds of canned foods.

The American family had a native cook when they were settled in the foreign country. The native cook liked to open the cans and prepare the food. But one evening there was a can that puzzled him. The native cook complained about it to the lady of the house.

The native cook told the lady that he had tried and tried to cook the food from this can. No matter how long the food was cooked it was still hard. No matter how much water was added the food was still hard. No matter how many spices he added, the food was still unable to be eaten.

The lady of the house was puzzled, too. She went into the kitchen to find out what had been in the can. She soon found out why the food was inedible. The can had contained four golf balls.

Apology Accepted

(Adapted from "Rotarian," Sept. 1940)

Mr. and Mrs. Smith had a four year old daughter. They took her with them on a visit to Mr. Smith's parents. While they were at the little girl's grandparents' house, the family doctor came in. The doctor was attracted to the little girl. He began to ask her a great many questions.

The little girl answered all of the questions very politely. After a while she began to get tired of answering his questions. She looked up into the doctor's face. In a very loud voice she said, "Oh, doctor, you're full of prunes!"

The father and mother of the little girl were embarrassed. They told the little girl she must apologize to the doctor at once. The little girl said she would apologize.

She walked over to the doctor and said, "Doctor, I'm very sorry that you are full of prunes."

Not So Foolish

A farmer once received fifty dollars in cash. It was the dividend on a life insurance policy. He took the fifty dollars and bought a cow.

When the farmer came home with the cow, his wife was disappointed. She said, "When you had the fifty dollars, why didn't you buy yourself a bicycle? That would be fine for you to ride back and forth on when you go to town. You need something like that. Just think how foolish you would look trying to ride down Main Street on a cow."

"Well," said the farmer, "we need more milk. I think I would look a lot more foolish trying to milk a bicycle."

PUBLICATIONS DESIGN, WASHINGTON, D. C.

DATE

JAN 07 '99

NOV 1 5 1993

OCT 3 1 1997

HIGHSMITH 45-220